GOLF'S SUPERSHOTS

Books by George Peper

Golf's Supershots, 1982
Scrambling Golf, 1977

GOLF'S
SUPERSHOTS

HOW THE PROS PLAYED THEM—
HOW YOU CAN PLAY THEM

by GEORGE PEPER

Illustrated by Ron Ramsey

Atheneum

New York

1982

Library of Congress Cataloging in Publication Data

Peper, George.
Golf's supershots.

1. Golf. I. Title.
GV965.P42 1982   796.352′3   81-66018
ISBN 0-689-11135-5   AACR2

Published simultaneously in Canada by McClelland and Stewart Ltd.
Manufactured by Halliday Lithograph Corporation,
West Hanover, Massachusetts
DESIGNED BY ROBERT MICHAELS
First Edition

For Libby and Timmy

Acknowledgments

The author is indebted in several ways and to many individuals. First, to the following authors, whose books provided invaluable background material: Billy Casper, *Golf Shotmaking with Billy Casper*; Robert Tyre (Bobby) Jones, Jr., *Bobby Jones on Golf* and *Golf Is My Game*; Michael McDonnell, *Golf: The Great Ones* and *Great Moments in Golf*; Johnny Miller, *Pure Golf*; Arnold Palmer, *Go for Broke!*; Gene Sarazen, *Thirty Years of Championship Golf*; Herbert Warren Wind, *The Story of American Golf*; and Mildred (Babe) Didriksen Zaharias, *Championship Golf*. Also, to Ken Bowden, a superlative editor, for his good advice and encouragement, and to artist Ron Ramsey, who draws the finest likenesses I've ever seen, for his patience and professionalism on the dozens of illustrations. Finally, special thanks go to each of the following players: Seve Ballesteros, Patty Berg, Billy Casper, Roberto de Vicenzo, Raymond Floyd, Hale Irwin, Tony Jacklin, Nancy Lopez-Melton, Johnny Miller, Jack Nicklaus, Byron Nelson, Jerry Pate, Gary Player, Sam Snead, Peter Thomson, Lee Trevino, Tom Watson and Mickey Wright, most of whom not only described their great shots in detail but offered instructional advice as well, and all of whom provided the book's inspiration.

Contents

Introduction

Bobby Jones, who wrote about golf even more ably than he played it, once made the following observation on his career: "The most acute and yet the most satisfying recollections I have are of the tournaments won by triumphs over my own mistakes and by crucial strokes, played with imagination and precision, when anything ordinary would not have sufficed."*

Jones was referring to the "supershots," those rare blends of mastery and magic that provide golf's greatest thrills. His own legendary career included several of them—a brilliant recovery from sand at Royal Lytham; a 230-yard four-iron at Winged Foot; a "scuttled" chip shot through the middle of a bunker at Scioto—each helping him to win one of his thirteen major championships.

And yet, Jones' words should strike a familiar chord with all golfers, regardless of ability. For each of us has, at one time or another, played a supershot. It may not have been recorded in the newspapers or marked by a bronze plaque, but surely it is engraved in our memory.

In my own case, three shots stand out: I have made a hole-in-one; I have intentionally caromed a ball off a tree to within inches of the hole; and I have eagled a par four by sinking a 170-yard shot from a fairway bunker. I remember each of those shots as if I'd hit them yesterday, even though all were played several years ago. Furthermore, I find it impossible to walk the holes on which those shots were played without replaying them in my mind, and, occasionally, boring my partners with lengthy, embellished tales of the great moments.

This book will spare you such autobiographical lore, but it does contain accounts of the most dramatic shots played by two

* From *Golf Is My Game*, by Robert Tyre (Bobby) Jones, Doubleday & Co., Inc., Garden City, New York, 1960.

dozen of the world's greatest golfers. Each of the players featured is a winner of a major championship, and most of them have won several majors. In fact, the majority of the supershots were played during the final holes of U.S. Opens, British Opens, PGA Championships and Masters tournaments.

Each of the twenty-four chapters is divided into two sections: the first part describes the great shot, and the second part offers practical instruction on how you can play similar shots from difficult situations. Since the historical anecdotes are extremely varied, the instruction covers every aspect of the game —driving, fairway woods, irons, maneuvering the ball, short game, sand play, trouble shots and putting. And although most of the how-to is geared toward any level of player, each chapter includes a special tip entitled "If You Dare," intended for better players and for those dire situations requiring an all-out effort.

Thus, while most golf instruction books tell you how to hit good shots, this one tells you how to play *great* ones. And why not—if you think about it, supershots are an important part of any amateur's game. Since he puts himself into difficult situations with great regularity, he should also know how to extricate himself.

When you play a good shot from a difficult, testing lie, you always save at least one stroke, and more often you save two or three. Play two such shots per round and your scores will quickly improve. The fact is that, except for putting, no part of your game deserves more attention than the supershots.

I hope this book will help you and entertain you at the same time.

George Peper
1982

GOLF'S SUPERSHOTS

JACK NICKLAUS
at the British Open

The power drive

Jack Nicklaus stood on the eighteenth tee of the Royal & Ancient Golf Club of St. Andrews and gazed solemnly down the fairway. For once in his life, he seemed uncertain.

It was 1970, the final moments of the eighteen-hole playoff between Nicklaus and Doug Sanders for the British Open. Twenty-four hours earlier Sanders had tossed away the title when he missed a three-foot putt on this same hole. Now they were back to the scene of the crime.

Taking advantage of the reprieve, Nicklaus had gained a four-stroke cushion through thirteen. At that point many of the spectators had begun to drift back to the grandstands at eighteen, in order to have a good view of Jack's acceptance speech.

But then the momentum shifted. Sanders holed birdie putts at fourteen and fifteen as Nicklaus made pars, and then, apparently unnerved by the uprising, Jack overshot the green at sixteen and bogeyed. Suddenly his lead was down to one, and that's how it stood on the eighteenth tee.

Sanders played first, and played beautifully. Using every millimeter of his abbreviated swing he spanked the ball deep down the center of the fairway, just short of the Valley of Sin, that sweeping depression thirty yards short of the final green.

Now it was Jack's move. He knew he could drive the ball onto the green 358 yards away—he had done it four days in a row in 1964, three times with a three-wood. He had done it a couple of times this week, too. The British ball seemed to sail particularly high and long under the force of his upright, powerful swing. Besides, the eighteenth at St. Andrews was, by his reckoning, one of the most vulnerable holes in golf.

But was it worth the risk? Even a slight mistake, a minutely off-center impact, and he could send the ball careening over the fence and into the old gray buildings lining the fairway, taking with it all hope of winning the championship. A cautious four-wood, a wedge and two putts would certainly tie Sanders, and probably beat him, and a one-putt birdie would lock it up. Truly there was little need to go for the green in one shot. Yet, if he knew he could do it, why not try?

Thousands of people lined the fairway and leaned from the windows of the buildings overlooking the course as Nicklaus pondered his dilemma.

For a while he did nothing but stare, a mixture of concentration and confoundedness in his smouldering blue eyes. Then he began to move, to grapple rather awkwardly in fact, until it became clear what he was doing. He was removing his V-neck sweater—the sure sign that he had decided to go for it all.

Nicklaus fingered his driver, took a couple of limbering practice swings, and then went to work, gathering himself for the most audacious teeshot of his career: He glanced at the target, then at the ball, then at his aim spot several feet forward on the tee, then back to the ball, all the while shifting his feet, securing his grip, getting comfortable. Finally, a pause and then the Nicklaus trigger, that slight turn of the head to the right. All at once arms and club were high in the sky, left heel off the ground and then back down again, his entire body flashing through the ball, uncoiling in an awesome explosion of power.

From the moment of impact, Jack knew his worst fears were over. He had launched the ball straight at the green with no drift to the right. But, as the ball continued to fly, a new fear crept in—it may have been hit *too* well.

"After I hit it I winced inside," recalls Nicklaus. "I said to myself, 'My God, you nailed it, you hit it too hard.' "

The ball was still hot when it bounded past Sanders' drive and raced through the Valley of Sin. It reached the green like a scared rabbit, scooting past the pin and up toward the gallery crowding the fence beyond a few feet of fringe grass. There, just a couple of feet short of out-of-bounds, it snagged in the heavy rough.

Nicklaus had risen to the occasion. Indeed, he had nearly risen beyond it.

Moments later both men wedged to within five feet of the hole. Nicklaus, playing first, stroked his slippery downhiller—and once again he applied too much power. He reached out in desperation as the ball began to slide out of his intended line. Then, unbelievably, it caught the edge of the hole and disappeared. The elated champion tossed his putter high in the air. He had won his second British Open, and won at the Home of Golf—one of his greatest ambitions. Eight years later he would return to St. Andrews, and win the world's oldest championship for a third time.

Hitting the Power Drive

Few golfers will ever hit a tee shot 360 yards as Nicklaus did, but most players can add distance by applying the proper techniques.

You can guarantee yourself a minimum of ten extra yards simply by standing up to the ball in a strong position. One of the keys to power is a strong left side, and you can preprogram that by addressing the ball so that the club and your left arm form a perfectly straight line, extending from the tip of your left shoulder to the ball. The right side should be "soft," with the right elbow tucked close to the body in a preview of its proper position at impact. The legs, containing your most powerful muscles, should be flexed and in a "ready" position, similar to the stance a swimmer takes before diving into a pool for a race. Your stance should be shoulder-width or slightly wider, to provide a broad, stable base and encourage a full swing arc.

Many players in search of extra distance make the mistake of standing farther away from the ball than they would for a normal shot. That position

Establish a strong left side, with your arm and the club extended in a straight line.

out and smack the ball—but it's absolutely wrong. Standing too far from the ball forces you into a stiff-legged position where you must bend deeply from the waist simply to reach the ball. The result is a swing made mostly with the hands and arms, containing only small

gives them the feeling they can reach muscles, rather than the powerful legs. A lot of distance is lost with that kind of swing, so don't stand back for the big hit.

However, you might want to experiment with the angling of your feet. Most of the better golfers stand Ben Hogan–style, with the right foot perpendicular to the target line and the left flared slightly toward the target. But if you flare that right foot just a bit, you'll find it gives you more flexibility on your backswing for a bigger turn, a better coil and, therefore, a more powerful forward swing. And if you increase the flare on the left foot, you may improve your ability to clear the left side during the downswing for a more powerful move into impact. Experiment with these foot positions to see which does the most for you. And in any case, never set up with both feet perpendicular to the target line—not if you want a big drive. Such a position robs you of balance and elasticity, and can take twenty-five yards off your tee shot.

One final piece of advice on setting up to the ball. At address—and throughout the swing—maintain a light grip pressure. Don't hold the club any more firmly than you would hold a ball you are about to throw. If you grip too tightly your whole body will tense up and you'll have great difficulty making the full, free swing necessary for a long drive. Also, if you hang on too tightly at address, you will tend to loosen your grip at the worst time, at the top of the swing, thereby losing control of the clubhead. However, if you maintain a light pressure at address, you'll have a good feel for the clubhead, and will respond at the top of the swing by firming your grip naturally as the centrifugal force pulls at your hands. That's the way it *should* be—and that is the way it *will* be if you hold the club lightly.

The two key takeaway words are "low and slow." Keeping the club low to the ground for at least the first fifteen inches of the backswing will help you make a wide, powerful arc. It will also facilitate a firm, one-piece takeaway, with the club, hands, arms and shoulders all turning away from the ball as one solid unit, and with no early cocking of the wrists.

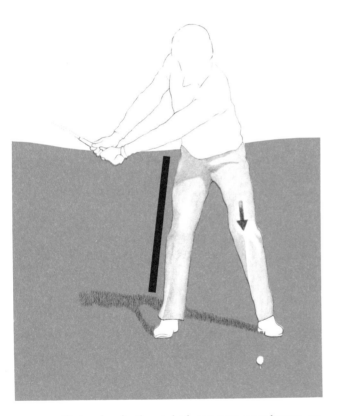

Going back, the right knee acts as a brace, as the left knee flexes toward the ball.

As you extend into the backswing be sure your right knee remains flexed yet firmly set as a brace against any lateral sway. At the same time, allow your left leg to move; it is the left knee that initiates the movement and coiling of the lower body. Halfway into the backswing, the left knee should be pointing directly at the ball as your arms and the club extend horizontally to the right.

The bigger your "coil" at the top, the more powerful your downswing will be. Some people can coil more easily than others simply because they have slimmer or more supple physiques. If you're muscular or thickly built through the upper torso, you can increase your coil by allowing your left heel to rise as you reach the top of the swing. For many years, this was thought to be poor form, but some of today's best players, Jack Nicklaus and Tom Watson included, lift the left heel on teeshots.

It's worthwhile to spend some time in front of a full-length mirror checking the following power points at the top of your swing. First, be sure that the right leg has continued to act as a brace and has allowed no lateral movement. Second, check that your left arm has not collapsed. If you have allowed the elbow to bend, it means you have let your swing become dominated by your arms and hands. You are swinging the club like an axe and will be prone to casting from the top with the hands rather than letting the lower body pull the upper body through the ball. So resist the temptation to let the left arm bend.

Be sure your grip, although light, is secure, particularly in the last three fingers of the left hand. If it loosens, the club will drop downward toward your shoulder a bit, giving the appearance of a long full backswing. But, in fact, such a position is sloppy at best, and it can precipitate a host of more serious errors on the downswing. Finally, ask yourself whether there is a feeling of tension in your shoulders and thighs. There should be. You should feel balanced and in control, yet taut and ready to unwind.

At the top: a braced right side, a raised heel, a straight left arm, a secure grip, a taut coil.

If you can achieve that tightly wound top-of-swing position, the downswing will take care of itself. Be aware, however, that a proper downswing proceeds from the bottom up. In the cases of Nicklaus and Watson, the downswing seems to begin with a slamming to the ground of that raised left heel just as the club reaches the end of its backswing. The lowering of the heel triggers a lateral movement of the knees, followed by a pull downward with the hands and the flashing through impact of the club in an explosion of centrifugal force timed precisely to coincide with the most powerful stage of the uncoiling process.

Although it's impossible to think about anything at impact, you should strive for a position in which the left side is as firm as it was at address and the right side is driving through the ball down along the target line and into an extension position that mirrors the half-way back position, with the arms and club pointing directly at the target, then floating upward into a full and unrestricted follow-through.

Practice all these positions—the address, takeaway, backward extension, top of swing, impact, forward extension and finish. If you can get the feel of each of them individually, you'll have an easier time putting them together in a single powerful motion.

One other point about the power drive: Don't try to use it on every tee. It's best to swing within yourself ninety-nine percent of the time, saving the big drive for occasions where you really need it, such as on short par-fives where a long teeshot might enable you to hit the green in two. Not even the tour's longest hitters swing all-out on every hole.

Finally, when you do go for the big ball, limber up. Just before taking the big cut, do yourself a favor and stretch your muscles a bit. Nicklaus is fond of hooking a club between his elbows and behind his back, then pivoting back and forth, stretching his leg and back muscles for a full shoulder turn. You should do the same; not only will it help you summon the long ball, it will prevent a pulled muscle or other injury.

IF YOU DARE: CARRY A BIG STICK

If you're happy with the way you're swinging at the ball but you're still not getting the distance you'd like, the answer may lie in changing drivers. Jack Nicklaus did this back in 1978, switching to a club with less loft, and went on to win his third British Open the same year.

If you play on a seaside course, or in Texas or Florida or elsewhere where the winds are strong, you may benefit from a strong-lofted driver, which will give you a lower, more boring trajectory. If you tend to fade and slice the ball, a driver with a slightly hooked face may also help. If you have a smooth swing, a lightweight graphite shaft could be the answer. And if you're a fast swinger you might get more distance by either trading up to a stiffer shaft or trying a heavier clubhead. Depending on other swing characteristics, you might add a few yards by changing the lie and/or length of your driver.

The best advice is to consult your local PGA professional. Ask him to give you the "specs" he feels you should be using, i.e., length, lie, loft, weight, swingweight, shaft stiffness and material, and then check his advice against the driver you're now playing. If you find big discrepancies, it's probably time to make a change.

ROBERTO DE VICENZO
at the Crosby

The driver from the fairway

If the Gods of Golf would allow each of us to select one spectacular hole on which to hit the shot of a lifetime, it's a good bet many of us would choose number eighteen at Pebble Beach. Stretched along 600 yards of California's most scenic coastline, this bedeviling par five has often been called the best finishing hole in golf.

And if, having chosen that hole, we could also call our ultimate shot, the selection would come quickly. For nearly all of us it would be the second shot, the long approach, hit low and hard and out over the edge of the Pacific. It would land just over the last guardian bunker, bound forward, and finish stiff to the wind-whipped flag, leaving a makeable putt for an eagle.

In the final round of the 1961 Bing Crosby National Pro-Am, Roberto de Vicenzo hit exactly that dream shot. What's more, he hit it in swashbuckling style—he pummeled the ball with a driver.

"I was paired with Bob Rosburg, who was leading me by two shots as we came to the eighteenth tee," recalls de Vicenzo. "Bob hit first, and placed his tee shot right where he wanted it, in the exact center of the fairway. From there he could protect his lead, but I knew he could never get to the green in two, even though we had a following wind.

"I also knew what I had to do if I wanted to have any chance of catching Rossy and winning the tournament—I had to eagle the hole. And I knew the only way I could do that was by hitting the green, by putting together two near-perfect shots. So I aimed my tee shot fifty yards left of where Bob had hit his. I aimed it out along the edge of the ocean, and I told myself to hit the ball as hard and as straight as I knew how."

The shot came off just as de Vicenzo wanted. Long and high, it sailed with the wind on a path that skirted the Pacific and rolled to a halt at the very corner of the dogleg. He was halfway home, with 270 yards left to the pin.

11

Moments later, Rosburg hit a three-iron to a point about a hundred yards short of the green. As de Vicenzo approached his ball, he knew only one club in the bag could get him home.

"Fortunately, I had a perfect lie," he recalls. "The ball was sitting up nicely, which was a good break, because I knew I would have to hit the driver again, even harder and straighter than I had from the tee. But I knew that if I could hit such a shot, my ball would reach the pin."

Few golfers of the modern era have struck the ball more squarely or with greater consistency than de Vicenzo, the comparatively unheralded winner of over 150 tournaments worldwide, including the 1967 British Open. On this shot, which called for the highest expression of his artistry, he responded with near perfection. Using the long, lazy swing that belied his immense power, de Vicenzo unleashed a missile. The ball beamed out over the ocean, over the jagged rocks, the seawall, the last stretch of fairway and finally over the greenside bunker. On the green, it took one big bounce and rolled to rest eight feet from the pin.

Rosburg, visibly shaken, left his relatively simple wedge shot forty feet short of the hole. Suddenly it looked as if de Vicenzo's dream scenario would be acted out. Two putts by Rossy, one by Roberto, and they would go to sudden death.

But it didn't happen. With the suddenness of an uppercut to the jaw, Rosburg rammed home his forty-footer for a birdie that clinched the victory.

De Vicenzo, the wind out of his sails, missed his eagle putt. He left the green runner-up. And yet he left it with the special knowledge that in the most demanding situation of his career he had responded with the most spectacular shot of his life.

The Tee-less Teeshot

The driver from the fairway is perhaps the only aggressive shot in golf that can be played more frequently by fifteen-handicappers than by professionals.

Fairways on the PGA Tour are cut so close and maintained so meticulously that the pros rarely get a "furry" lie, where the ball sits up high above the level of the turf, allowing solid impact with the deep-faced, low-lofted driver. Instead, the tour pros invariably get very "tight" lies, where the ball sits close to the top of the grass. Gen-

Your first step is to read the lie. If at least part of the ball is above the top of your driver, it's a smart shot. If the ball sits well below the top, look out. Anywhere in between, you're gambling.

erally that's the way they like it for crisp iron shots, but tight fairway lies do not encourage the use of the driver.

Furthermore, the pros rarely *need* to use a driver from the fairway; they hardly ever require that much distance, except on the mid-length par-five holes that they want to reach in two shots, as in the case of de Vicenzo at Pebble Beach.

For amateurs, however, the driver from the fairway can be a handy and often-used shot. Most amateurs do not play on tour-caliber courses, so furry and perched lies are far more common. Also, in spring and fall many courses allow winter rules, permitting players to place the ball in a perfect lie. Such conditions not only allow use of the driver, they encourage it. Finally, the rough on many courses is short, sparse and often dried out. If you get a perched lie in those conditions, it is ideal for a driver. In fact, when the ball is perched in light rough and you have a long, open path to the green, it is foolish to play any club *but* the driver.

The most important key in hitting the shot is a mental one—you must be able to distinguish "friendly" lies from unfriendly ones. You can do so simply by lightly soling the driver in back of the ball, and comparing that visual impression to your address position when the ball sits on a tee. If the top of your driver is almost even with the equator of the ball (as it should be when you have the ball teed on a peg) you have an ideal lie for a tee-less teeshot. If less than half the ball is above the top of your driver, be careful —or, at least, be confident of your swing—because you'll be taking a chance unless you are a five-handicapper or better. If the top of the driver is even with or above the top of the ball, put the driver back in the bag and take out a more lofted club.

To hit with the driver from the fairway, you should make a couple of minor adjustments and then just follow the fundamentals for playing a solid teeshot.

First, to be sure you stay down to the ball, flex your knees a bit more than you normally do at address. As you do so, loosen your hold on the club and choke down the same amount that you flex your knees—just an inch or so. From this position you'll be better able to make a controlled swing while staying low to the ball.

Set up as you would for a tee shot, with the ball off your left heel, most of your weight right.

The ball should be positioned as it would be on a regular tee shot—off your left heel-to-instep—and you should feel that at least sixty percent of

The downswing key is to resist the "hit impulse." Sweep into the back of the ball.

your weight is on your right foot. This will encourage you to make the most important move for this shot—a long, low, one-piece takeaway. It is crucial to keep the clubhead low to the ground for the first foot or so of the takeaway. If you take the club back low, you will swing it through impact in the same manner, sweeping the clubhead squarely into the back of the ball.

Above all, keep your swing controlled. You probably should not let the club get even parallel to the ground at the end of your backswing unless you're playing from an absolutely perfect lie. And the smooth, deliberate pace of your takeaway should be retained, even as you move into the downswing. Bobby Jones once observed that everyone is so preoccupied with the slow backswing that they forget about the importance of proper pace in the most vital part of the swing, the first move down. Jones advocated making the first move down a slow one, just as slow as the takeaway. That key is more important than ever when playing a driver from the fairway. So resist the "hit impulse" as best you can, and just let the clubhead sweep through the ball.

After all, you don't have to slash at the ball when the club in your hands is a driver.

IF YOU DARE: DRIVERS THAT "MOONLIGHT"

Just as there are drivers designed for maximum distance, there are drivers that are ideal for playing shots from the fairway. As you might imagine, a weak-lofted club (one with about thirteen degrees of loft) is easier to wield than a strongly lofted one (with ten degrees or less). Even more important is the depth of the clubface. If it is shallow (short from the top to bottom of the face) you'll be better able to make contact with the bottom of the ball than if you have a deep-faced driver (large from top to bottom). Sole-weighted and backweighted drivers also aid in getting the ball airborne. Finally, you might consider replacing your driver with a two-wood. You will lose a few yards off the tee, but you'll make up for it with increased accuracy and greater aggressiveness from the fairway and light rough.

RAYMOND FLOYD
at the Masters

Hilly lies

"When he's hot, he's unbeatable."

The comment was made by Jack Nicklaus; the man he was describing was Raymond Floyd. Nicklaus' appraisal came at the end of four days in April 1976, when Floyd was as hot as any player has ever been in a major championship.

After seventy-two holes over the Augusta National Golf Club course, Floyd posted a score of 271, tying the seventeen-under-par mark set eleven years earlier by Nicklaus himself. Floyd led that Masters championship from wire to wire, and won by a record eight shots. Throughout the four days of competition no one even threatened him.

Floyd has often credited his success that week to his mastery of the fairway woods, particularly the five-wood, which he had added to his bag just one week before the tournament. He used the woods primarily on Augusta National's par-five holes: numbers two, eight, thirteen and fifteen. In his four trips through those holes

Floyd notched an incredible twelve birdies, one eagle and three pars, for a record fourteen-under-par on the long holes alone.

Nearly every time he played a par-five he reached it in two. His teeshot invariably finished not simply in the fairway, but on the precise plateau, sector and patch of grass that afforded the best shot to the green. In only one instance, in fact, did he drive the ball into anything less than Position A+, and it was on that occasion that, Floyd claims, he played the most ambitious approach of his life.

"Actually, at the time I didn't think the shot was risky at all," recalls Floyd, "but a week later, when I saw some videotapes of the tournament, I couldn't believe my eyes. I should never have attempted the shot I played. It just shows how positive my thinking was that week."

It happened in the third round on number thirteen. Floyd, hoping to draw his teeshot around the crook of this lovely right-to-left dogleg hole, instead pushed it slightly, and his ball finished near the base of one of two tall Georgia pines which mark the corner of the hole. Not a bad drive, to be sure, but hardly a great one. For one thing, he was precisely in the "decision zone," where a player must choose either to go for the green, risking a carry of more than 200 yards over menacing Rae's Creek, or to play a middle iron safely short of the creek, then wedge on for a sure par or a one-putt birdie. To compound the problem, Floyd had a steep sidehill lie, with the ball nearly a foot above his stance.

But there was never a question in Raymond's mind. He would go for it. "The pin that day was cut severely front-right," he recalls, "meaning if I were to lay up I'd have to hit a perfect little cut shot over the creek in order to keep the ball close to the hole. I remember telling myself that, if I could hit the five-wood as well as I had been hitting it all week, I'd carry the ball into the left trap, and from there I could easily make par, and possibly birdie. It was a long carry for a five-wood—about 210 yards into the wind—but I was swinging so well I felt I could make it."

At that moment in the championship, Floyd's lead was more fragile than it had been all week—just three shots over a momentarily charging Hubert Green. And Floyd had just made his only double-bogey of the tournament two holes earlier when his approach to the eleventh hole found water. A similar result from this five-wood would undoubtedly mean bogey or worse, and would change the complexion of the tournament. This was a shot Floyd *had* to execute if he was to keep the magic alive.

And he did it. "As my club struck the ball," Floyd says, "I thought, 'My God, you've flushed it—you've hit it too well. It'll go over the sand and into the heavy grass.' But I was wrong. In fact, the ball barely reached the bunker."

From there, Floyd (one of the tour's finest sand players) executed a near-perfect shot and sank a tap-in for the tenth of his twelve birdies. Suddenly, his lead was five shots. It would never be smaller.

Handling Hilly Lies

Since you're likely to encounter at least one or two hilly lies every time you play, it pays to know how to handle them. Basically, there are four types: uphill, downhill, sidehill with the ball above your feet (as was Floyd's) and sidehill with the ball below your feet. The sidehill lies are the trickiest, so we'll look at them first.

Sidehill lie with the ball above the feet:

When asked how he adjusted to the uneven lie, Floyd said he played it "naturally," without thinking too much about mechanics. That's fine for a tour player, but most of us have neither the talent nor the experience of Raymond Floyd. Therefore, it pays to make a few adjustments. After a bit of practice these will become as natural to you as they were to Floyd.

When the ball is above your feet it's also closer to your hands, causing you to feel crowded, so in taking your stance you tend to "uncrowd" yourself by standing farther away from the ball than normal—too far away, in most cases. This position may feel good, but it isn't. It forces you to reach outward to the ball, and sets you up for a swing that is so flat you will rarely make solid contact with the ball. Instead, you will tend either to pull the ball to the left or hook it.

To counteract this "uncrowding" reaction, make a conscious effort not to stand too far from the ball. Let your arms hang naturally from your shoulders to the grip of the club—in other words, don't reach for the ball. Also, to compensate for the nearness of the ball, grip down at least an inch or two on the club.

You will probably have a tendency when swinging to fall backward on your heels, so at address try to put slightly more weight than usual on your toes. This will help you to contact the ball a bit earlier in the swing, before the clubface has had a chance to close, so that you won't be as likely to hook or pull the ball to the left.

Since all hilly lies require firm balance, shorten your backswing to three-quarter length, and concentrate on making a smooth, unhurried swing. Finally, no matter what you do, you will probably see some degree of right-to-left drift, so allow for this by aiming a few yards right of your target.

Sidehill lie with ball below feet:

This is occasionally referred to as "the shank lie." When the ball is below the feet, it is farther from the hands than normal, so you tend to stand closer to the ball to get the same feel as on a level shot. However, such an adjustment simply moves your entire swing plane out toward the ball an inch or so, resulting in the swing becoming more upright and your body tending to fall forward toward the ball because of distorted balance. Even if you tip just a little, it's enough to bring the club into impact an inch or so outside its usual path so that you contact the ball with the hosel of the club. The result is a shank.

A couple of quick adjustments will eliminate the shanks and facilitate solid shots from this lie. First, take at

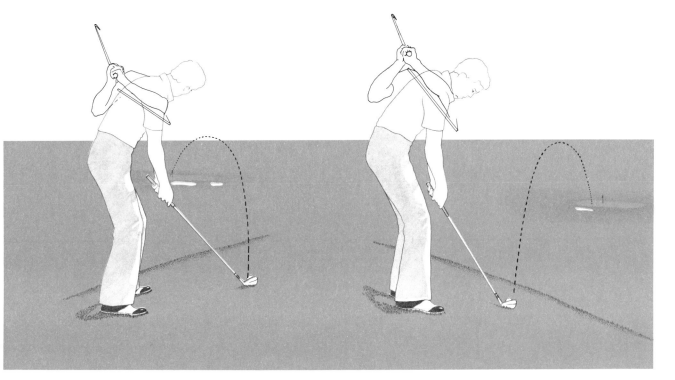

When the ball is above your feet, grip down on the club and keep most of your weight on your toes. When it's below your feet, widen your stance, shade your weight to your heels and take extra club.

least one more club than you would from a level lie. Play a five-iron, for example, instead of a six. Since it's important to stay in balance, you don't want to have to swing hard with any club; it's wiser to make a smooth pass with a longer club. Also, you will probably fade the ball from this lie, and the fade reduces distance, so you should compensate by using plenty of stick.

As with the opposite sidehill shot, take an address posture which lets your arms and hands hang naturally from your shoulders. (Don't get yourself into an overly erect "Don January" position.) Also, widen your stance an inch or two. This will inhibit unnecessary leg movement, increase your balance and bring your hands lower to the ball, thereby reducing the chance of a topped or whiffed shot.

Since your weight will tend to drift out toward the toes, balance yourself at address by distributing most of your weight on your heels. Be sure that you are "down" to the ball by bending a little from the waist. It's not necessary to flex the knees too much.

From this position, using a deliberate three-quarter swing, you will not only avoid the shank, you will hit a solid shot every time. The only other adjustment is to aim a few yards left to compensate for the inevitable fade.

Uphill lie:

Most golfers agree that this is the easiest of the uneven lie situations. In fact, the beginning player often hits the ball more solidly from an uphill lie than from level ground, the main reason being that there is a certain amount of loft built in. From this lie, it is almost impossible to top the ball.

On the other hand, it's difficult to hit a shot long and straight from an uphill lie without making a couple of changes in your setup. First, be aware of the flight characteristics of shots from this lie. You'll tend to hit the ball much higher than from a level lie, and you'll also tend to pull or hook it to the left. You can guard against the increased height, and accompanying loss of distance, by taking one club more than normal—and even, on severely steep hills, perhaps two clubs more. To counteract the leftward drift, aim your toe line, knees, hips and shoulders a few yards right of your target.

On markedly uphill lies it's also a good idea to play the ball a little forward of its normal position in your stance, which, for most players, will mean somewhere forward of the left heel on long shots, opposite the left heel on shorter shots. To maintain your balance, make your hips parallel to the slope by flexing your left knee slightly. This will put more weight on your left side and thereby protect you from falling down the slope as you shift the weight in your backswing.

The swing should be extra smooth and slow. Take the club back straight down the slope; this will insure that you swing it straight up the slope and solidly into the back of the ball at impact. Don't swing back farther than three-quarter length. Remember, you have at least one club more than usual so you don't have to make a big turn. If you overswing you risk falling off the ball to the right. If you execute properly, you'll get a high, soft draw—one of the prettiest shots in golf.

Downhill lie:

As you might expect, the flight characteristics of shots from this lie are exactly opposite to those of shots from uphill lies. The ball will fly on a relatively low trajectory and will invariably drift from left to right.

You can compensate for the lack of

loft by taking one *less* club than usual, a six-iron, for instance, instead of a five. Don't worry about the loss of distance; the lower trajectory will make the ball fly almost as far as a five-iron from a level lie. Besides, if the ground slopes downward all the way to the green, you don't *need* as much club as you do on a level fairway. Remember also that, should you land short of the green, you can expect plenty of bounce and roll from a downward-sloping landing area. In fact, in such situations it's best to land the ball short of the green, assuming no hazards guard its approach.

The best way to compensate for the inevitable left-to-right curve is simply to aim a few yards left of your target and then let your shot drift toward the pin. Set yourself squarely to the ball, flexing your right knee slightly more than normal—this should make your hips parallel to the slope. Next, take a couple of practice swings to determine proper ball position. You'll probably find that the club clips the grass about a ball-width to the right of its normal position in your stance, so set up accordingly, with the ball slightly in back of its usual place. Also, shade your weight a little bit to the right. This will give you a "head start" on the weight shift you must make in the backswing and will also help you to get the ball airborne.

As with the uphill lie, the swing from the downhill lie must be smooth and controlled, no longer than three-quarter length. Use mostly the arms in leading the club up the slope on the backswing. Then let the legs move freely down the slope and through the ball, leading the arms and club back down the slope. You may have a tendency to fall forward and down the slope in your follow-through, but on this shot that's not a bad thing because it's an indication that you've stayed down and through the shot. In fact, if you visualize the finish that Gary Player sometimes makes—stepping forward after impact—and then try to duplicate it, you'll probably hit a very solid shot.

IF YOU DARE: WORK THE BLADE FOR STRAIGHT SHOTS

Let's say you have a lie similar to the one Ray Floyd had, with the ball well above your feet. Let's assume, further, that you have no room to hit the ball to the left, as Floyd did, nor do you have room to play a big draw because there are trees close to you on the right side. You must hit a straight ball from this position, which encourages pulls and hooks.

Your solution is in the way you point the clubface. If you have a shot of six-iron length, take a five-iron but open the face of the club. Assuming you do everything else correctly, this open-faced five-iron will give you a straight shot that will have the trajectory of a six-iron.

The reverse applies when you have a sidehill lie with the ball below your feet. If you can't afford to fade the ball or push it to the right, take one club less and close the blade. For a six-iron shot, take a seven-iron and toe it in at address. Then just follow the necessary adjustments, and you'll get a straight shot to the green.

ARNOLD PALMER
at the PGA

The wood from rough

On a wall in Arnold Palmer's office in Latrobe, Pennsylvania, is a small plaque bearing a poem. One of the verses reads:

> Life's battles don't always go
> To the stronger or faster man
> But sooner or later the man who
>   wins
> Is the man who thinks he can.

The words are by a little-known English poet, but they could have been written by Palmer himself. Never has the game seen a more confident, more aggressive champion.

"You must play boldly to win," said Palmer time and again. And time and again he proved it. At Cherry Hills. At Birkdale. At Troon. And at Augusta, four times.

Whereas most of golf's finest players could contend with do-or-die situations when they had to, Palmer built his entire game around them. He utterly depended on his daring style of play. Sometimes he died by his own

bold hand, but more often he charged his way to first place.

Yet, ironically, the single most electrifying shot of Palmer's career failed to bring him victory, a victory he wanted more than any other.

It happened in the PGA, the one major championship Palmer has not won. The year was 1968; the site, Pecan Valley Country Club in San Antonio, Texas. With one hole left to play, Palmer trailed Julius Boros by a shot.

The eighteenth at Pecan Valley is a 470-yard par-four dogleg right. A creek crosses the fairway roughly 245 yards from the green, forcing even the best players to lay up on the drive and then sting a long-iron to the elevated, blind green. It is the hardest hole on the course, and in that 1968 PGA championship, under a four-day assault from scores of the nation's best professionals, it yielded only nineteen birdies.

Palmer needed one of those birdies desperately. Boros, a two-time U.S.

Open champion, was playing just behind him and could not be expected to bogey the hole. Arnold had to take command.

He lashed into that final drive with extra fury—perhaps too much so, for the ball hooked into the heavy rough 230 yards from the green.

Somehow Arnold's next swing would have to move the ball out of the grass, across the creek, up the hill, onto the green and into a position from which he could make a birdie three. An impossible assignment, and yet just the kind of challenge Palmer enjoyed.

With a hitch of the pants and a glance at the green, Arnie drew his three-wood from the bag and waded into position. His massive arms and shoulders twisting and then untwisting around a rock-steady head, then exploding at once into a high, bell-tolling finish, Palmer virtually ripped the ball out of the grass and up the fairway on a low, slightly hooking path. It landed just short of the green and bounded forward onto the putting surface and up a hogback where, unbelievably, it hit the pin, caroming eight feet past the hole.

A roar erupted from the thousands surrounding the green. Surely this would be Arnie's greatest victory. Back down the fairway Boros had hit a short tee shot so he could not reach the green in two. He would have to one-putt for par, and, if he didn't, the title would go to Palmer, who certainly would roll in the putt. That would be the finale.

Palmer recalls the way it actually went: "The grass on that green was a particularly tough hybrid of Bermuda grass that was tougher and grainier than the customary Bermuda. It was grown to be long and strong in hot weather and it had been very hot that week in San Antonio. I hit the putt just

the way I wanted, but it didn't break a fraction of an inch. The grass just didn't give. The ball hung hole high while I saw the ultimate chance for this one title that so long eluded me—the PGA—slip just a little farther away."

Moments later, Boros made his one-putt par and won the championship.

Woods from Rough

Most beginning golfers follow a familiar pattern in dealing with rough. At first they try fairway woods from all sorts of lies, basing their club selection solely on distance from the green. Then, after painful experience convinces them the woods are not always the best choice, they overcompensate and avoid these power clubs entirely. Instead, they try to play long-iron shots

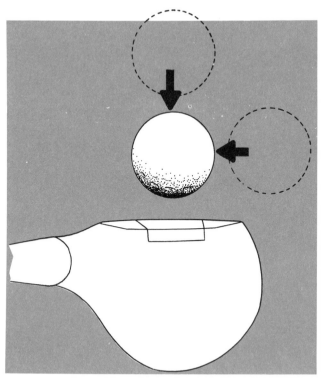

When in rough, play the ball a ball-width closer and a ball-width farther back than usual.

from heavy grass. Invariably they fail.

The truth is that it's easier to play shots from rough with fairway woods than with long-irons. When you have a good to moderate lie and you need the distance, a four- or five-wood is better than any iron in the bag. The reason is in the design of the clubs. The irons are relatively small and lightheaded, and, although they look as if they can slice through tall grass, they are comparatively ineffective in rough. Grass wraps around the hosel of the iron and twists the clubface, making clean, solid impact nearly impossible. Also, an iron club sometimes tends to dig down and under the ball in heavy rough, resulting in a heavy or fat shot that fails to carry the required distance.

The woods, on the other hand, have heavy, rounded heads which glide easily through the grass and cleanly into the ball, with no twisting or digging. The trick is in knowing when you can use, let's say, a five-wood instead of playing safe with a five-iron. No one can tell you this because each lie is different. However, it's safe to say that if the ball is down deep in the grass you'll have plenty of trouble with a wood. Also, if the grass is wet, the shot will be even tougher. If the grass is wiry Bermuda and/or growing against the path of your intended shot, it will also argue against a wood. But if you have a relatively good lie in dry grass, even heavy grass, go ahead with a fairway wood.

A wood shot from the rough must be played differently than a wood from the fairway. In the latter case you want a sweeping swing with the clubhead making a horizontal approach to the back of the ball. From the rough you need a more vertical descent to the ball in order to minimize the amount of grass between it and the clubhead, and

to help encourage the type of shot that ascends quickly and cleanly from the grass. You should try to contact the ball just before the clubhead reaches the absolute bottom of its swing arc.

You can preprogram the necessary swing at address. Set up with a slightly open stance—toeline, knees, hips, and shoulders all aligned a few yards left of your intended target. Play the ball back in your stance a bit more than you would on a fairway wood shot; just in back of the left heel is correct for most players. This should leave your hands slightly forward of the ball, a position which will encourage a downward blow.

Also, play the ball an inch or so closer to your feet than you normally would. It will feel a little strange, but it will help to give you the necessary more upright swing (the closer you stand to the ball, the more upright your swing plane will become).

As you take your address, do not ground your club behind the ball, because you might dislodge it from its lie, which would cost you a penalty stroke. Beyond this, if you keep your club just above the back of the ball you will force yourself to lift the club up sooner on the takeaway, which will help create a more upright swing. Finally, by keeping the club above the ball you will eliminate the chance of snagging the club in the grass as you take it back.

Once you've set up in this manner most of the work is done. From this position, simply make your own best swing, being sure to come down and through the ball firmly with your hands leading the club. There's no need to swing hard, but you must be *firm* on the way down, and you must *finish* the shot. If you do both you'll get plenty of distance—in most cases more distance than you would on a shot from the fairway.

From extra heavy rough, put slightly more flex in the knees and grip down on the club.

It's important to stay down on this shot, so maintain the knee flex throughout impact.

When you're in extra tough rough but you still want distance, stay with your wood but concentrate hard on a couple of things. First, use your legs. Put a little extra flex in the knees at address, and think of firing them toward the target as you begin your forward swing. Secondly, grip down a bit on the club. This will compensate for the lowering of your center of gravity which takes place when you flex your knees, but, more importantly, it will allow you to swing a little harder and still maintain control. Sometimes the answer to getting out of heavy rough is simply to swing forcefully. So flex the knees, grip down and swing hard.

And, remember—if you think you can play the shot, you probably can.

IF YOU DARE: PUNCH IT OUT

It's gratifying to muscle the ball out of rough and onto the green as Palmer did, but sometimes it's even more rewarding to "finesse" a shot from the rough. If you have a lofted fairway-wood—a five, six, or seven—try learning to punch the ball short distances to the green. A soft punch shot, even with a five-wood, can be more effective than beating on a six-iron. Grip way down (three to four inches) on the club, open your stance, and play the ball a bit forward of its usual position. Then make a low, short (three-quarter), firm-wristed backswing, using mostly the arms and shoulders, and punch through the ball. Don't let your arms and club go past parallel in the follow-through. The result should be a soft, low-flying punch. Distance is easy to control simply by shortening or lengthening your backswing. With a little practice this can be a useful shot from distances of 100 to 175 yards.

GENE SARAZEN
at the Masters

The long carry over water

It has been nearly fifty years since the stroke was played, but Gene Sarazen's double eagle in the 1935 Masters remains the most spectacular shot in the history of golf. The incredible four-wood that carried Rae's Creek and rolled into the fifteenth hole enabled Sarazen to catch Craig Wood, whom he beat the next day in an eighteen-hole playoff.

In his book, *Thirty Years of Championship Golf*, Sarazen gave a vivid description of "The Shot Heard Round the World."

• • •

I was anxious to make a creditable showing in my first Masters, for a representative group of champions, the old and the new, had been invited, and the old master himself (Bobby Jones) was competing. The experts didn't think that Bob could win. He had been away from tournament golf for over four years, and that's too long a time for even the greatest of golfers. Jones went for the highest price, though, in the Calcutta betting pool, with Craig Wood and myself also installed as fa-

vorites on the basis of form we had shown tuning up.

My practice rounds, 65, 67, 72 and 67, represented straight hitting and accurate putting on the sharply contoured greens. I was using a Cash-in putter, and the stroke I was getting with that model seemed to be precisely what was needed on the rye and Bermuda greens. I was also very pleased with the caddy assigned me, a lanky Negro well over six feet tall who had been nicknamed "Stovepipe" because of the battered tall silk hat he always wore when caddying. He was a very religious fellow and devoted a lot of his time to church activities. "Stovepipe," I used to ask him, "how are things going?" "Not so good, Mister Gene, not so good," he would drawl mournfully. "Collections were mighty poor today. We done got to win."

It was very cold for April in Georgia, the week of the Masters, but the scoring was torrid. Henry Picard opened with 67—68 before striking a rough third round of 76. Picard's 211 at the fifty-four-hole mark

From the book, *Thirty Years of Championship Golf* by Gene Sarazen with Herbert Warren Wind © 1950, renewed in 1978 by Prentice-Hall, Inc. Published by Prentice-Hall, Inc., Englewood Cliffs, New Jersey 07632 placed him two strokes behind the leader, Craig Wood. Wood, the golfer who looks like a tennis player, had fashioned three handsome rounds of 69, 72 and 68. That was too hot for me. I had held my practice form with 68, 71 and 73, in that order, but I trailed Wood by three shots and Picard by one.

The night before the final day's play I was cutting across the lobby of the Bon-Air Hotel, heading for the elevators and an early-to-bed, when I ran into Bob Davis, my old globetrotting friend. "Think you can catch 'em tomorrow?" Bob asked. Well, the way Craig was going, it was going to be a stiff assignment, but with a little luck I might still do it. "I've got just what you need," Bob said with a dramatic inflection. He slid an elaborate ring from his finger and placed it in my palm. "Gene, this was given to me by a dear friend of mine in Mexico City. It's a lucky ring. Juarez was wearing it when he was murdered." I said I didn't see what was so lucky about that. "Don't worry, just wear it," Bob retorted. I told him I couldn't wear it because it would interfere with my grip, but that I'd carry it in my pocket.

On the last round I was paired with Walter Hagen. Walter was out of the running and in a mood for reminiscing about the good old days—how he had sent a wheelchair out on the course for me when I was straggling home in the 1933 U.S. Open; how I had scoured St. Andrews later that year to find a similar chair or taxi or a perambulator to help an exhausted Hagen limp into port in the British; how he had kept the Prince of Wales and President Harding waiting, and so on. We were followed by a sparse gallery, for the bulk of the spectators were watching either Jones or Wood and Picard, who were playing together three holes or so ahead of us. It was about five-thirty in the afternoon when Walter and I came to the fifteenth hole. Both of us lined out good drives, mine being exceptionally long as I had a tail-end hook on it and the ground was hard. As we were walking to our balls, an ear-splitting roar erupted from the gallery jammed around the eighteenth green watching

Wood and Picard finish. It wasn't long before the news trickled down the valley: Wood had holed a birdie three on the 72nd hole for a total of 282. Picard was 286. As we neared the crest of the hole I squinted at the clubhouse in the distance, where photographers were snapping pictures of the happy winner and the newspapermen were hurrying to bat out their stories on Craig's victory.

Hagen played his second short of the pond that guards the approach to the green on the 485-yard fifteenth. I stopped for a moment and asked Stovepipe what I needed to win. "What do you mean, boss, to beat Craig Wood?" Stovepipe asked. I nodded. Hagen began to titter. "Oooh!" Stovepipe groaned, as he checked our round, "you need four 3's, Mister Gene, 3, 3, 3, 3."

I did some calculating. I could possibly get a birdie four on the fifteenth . . . maybe a birdie two on the sixteenth . . . and then maybe a birdie three on either the seventeenth or the eighteenth, which would give me a tie.

My high-flying optimism received a sudden jolt when I saw my lie. It was none too good. I went into a huddle with Stovepipe as to whether I should play a three-wood or a four-wood. The three, we decided, would never get the ball up from that close lie, being slightly deeper in the face than the four. The four, a new model called the Turfrider, had a hollow-back sole which enabled the club to go down after the ball. I knew that the only way I could reach the green with the four would be to toe the club in to decrease the loft and so give me extra yardage.

After it was settled that I would go with the four, I must have been scanning the skies for some sign of approval or encouragement, for I was suddenly reminded of the lucky ring Bob Davis had given me. I extracted it from my pocket and rubbed it over Stovepipe's head to give its reputed powers every chance to go to work. I suppose the real contribution the ring made was that fooling with it tapered off the tension that had been building up in me. I took my stance with my four-wood and rode into the shot with every ounce of strength and timing I could muster. The split second I hit the ball I knew it would carry the pond. It tore for the flag on a very low trajectory, not more than thirty feet in the air. Running forward to watch its flight, I saw the ball land on the green, still dead on line. I saw it hop straight for the cup, and then while I was straining to see how close it had finished, the small gallery behind the green let out a terrific shout and began to jump wildly in the air. I knew then that the ball had gone into the hole.

● ● ●

Woods Over Water

It is highly unlikely that the lucky ring used by Gene Sarazen possessed any magic powers, but it did help him "taper off the tension," and that in itself is quite a trick. The long approach over water is really no different from any shot with a long-iron or fairway wood, but it demands a full measure of calmness and self-assurance from anyone who decides to play it. So, under the assumption that you do not carry a magic ring, here are some tips that will help you to make a confident swing.

First, do your homework. Know what distance you hit each of your clubs—the carrying distance of your average shot, not the carry-plus-roll

distance of your best shot. The difference can be twenty yards or more. You can determine your distances by going to a practice tee at a time when no one is there, and hitting balls with each club. Hit at least a dozen shots, then step off the distance to where most of them land (on the longer clubs, you may have to estimate the amount of roll you must subtract). Again, be sure to record the distance of your *average* shot, not where the best shots finished.

Knowing your capabilities with each club from the wedge through the driver will help you on all your shots, but particularly on shots that call for a carry over a hazard. You will derive a large measure of the necessary confidence simply in knowing that you have the ideal club in your hand. Thus, if you have a carry of 200 yards, and you know that your average four-wood shot carries 205, you can swing away with the knowledge that, even if you hit a slightly below average shot, you'll be dry.

When you find that a carrying distance is in between clubs, you should always go for the longer club, both for the reason above and so you can make a smooth, unhurried swing at the ball.

Another way to reduce tension before swinging is to pick the "easiest" target. Normally, on a carry of 200 yards or more, you should not focus on the flagstick. Your main objective should be to put the ball on dry land and in a good position for your next shot, be that a pitch, a chip or a putt. So if, for example, the lake is wider on the left than on the right, as is the case at the fifteenth at Augusta, you should probably aim your shot a little to the right, assuming that the landing area is equally inviting left and right. By selecting the easier route, you'll reduce the pressure and this, too,

	Average Distance	
Club	Men	Women
3 wood	220 yds	170 yds
4 wood	190 yds	160 yds
3 iron	170 yds	140 yds
4 iron	160 yds	130 yds
5 iron	150 yds	120 yds
6 iron	140 yds	110 yds

will contribute to a smooth, confident swing.

The technical adjustments for this shot are relatively few, and, as with the mental ploys, they are geared to help you relax and swing with assurance. Mostly, they come under the heading "Don'ts":

- Don't change your stance. Set up square to the target, with the ball positioned off your left instep.
- Don't tense up on your grip. Keep a relatively light grip pressure, which will help you make a full and free-flowing swing.
- Don't stiffen your arms, as is the tendency on difficult long shots. Instead, let the arms hang naturally from the shoulders.
- Don't straighten your legs; if anything, put a little extra flex in the knees so that you stay down to

the ball and avoid the dreaded topped shot.

Since this shot demands a sweeping type of impact, concentrate on making a long, low takeaway and a good extension with the arms. Halfway into your backswing, your arms should stretch horizontally outward and directly away from your target. Your right hand and thumb should be in a "hitchhiker" position.

As you come out of impact, you should strive for the mirror image of that backswing position, this time with the left hand in the hitchhiker position. Good extension back and through will help give you a wide swing arc for plenty of power, and will encourage that low, sweeping impact that is essential to the success of this shot.

Make a long, low takeaway, stretching your arms into a full extension away from the target.

Post-impact is a mirror of the backswing extension, with the left hand in a "hitchhiker" position.

IF YOU DARE: GO FOR THE FLAG

Getting across the water is really only the first part of the "Sarazen shot." The other part is getting the ball to your objective. Sometimes, you want the ball to roll after clearing the water; in other instances you want it to sit. Depending on which of these results you're after, you should vary your club selection and your techniques.

If you want a rolling shot, the long iron is usually the best club, assuming you can handle your one-, two-, three-irons well, you have the proper lie and the distance is within your range. The long iron will give you a generally low trajectory and, unless you hit them the way Jack Nicklaus does, relatively little backspin. To give yourself even more roll, play the ball about a ball-width back of its normal position in your stance. This will give you an even lower trajectory and even less backspin; just be sure you allow yourself enough height to clear the hazard.

For a higher shot with less roll, the lofted five-, six-, or seven-woods are often the answer, especially if the lie is less than perfect. You should play the ball a ball-width forward of your usual position, open your stance and open the clubface to the target—not much, just a couple of degrees. As you come into impact, try to feel as if you are holding back the release of your wrists—essentially "blocking-out" the shot—keeping the clubface square to your target as you swing your arms and lower body through the ball. This is sometimes called "staying under the shot." You should get a high-floating ball that will land softly and with almost no roll.

HALE IRWIN
at the U.S. Open

The long iron

In 1980, shortly after he had won both the U.S. Open and the PGA Championship, Jack Nicklaus was asked to rate several of the courses he had played during his eighteen years as a professional. Using a scale of one to ten, with ten being the most difficult, Nicklaus responded this way:

> *Augusta National:* "That's an eight, maybe eight and a half."
> *Baltusrol:* "I guess that might be a ten."
> *Pebble Beach:* "That's a ten, too."
> *Oak Hill:* "An eight."
> *St. Andrews:* "It has great holes and poor holes—it's an eight."
> *Seminole:* "Between seven and eight."
> *Winged Foot:* "Winged Foot? Eleven, maybe twelve."

The greatest golfer in the game rated the West Course at Winged Foot Golf Club his toughest challenge, then added, "Of course, that's based on my last experience there."

He was referring to the 1974 U.S. Open, "The Massacre at Winged Foot."

It was the Open in which Nicklaus started with four straight bogeys. It was the Open in which the defending champion, Johnny Miller, made seven on a par three. It was the Open in which Arnold Palmer challenged for the last time, then faded with a final round of 76. And it was the Open in which Tom Watson challenged for the first time, and also crumbled on Sunday with a 79.

In the end there was only one real winner—Winged Foot. The course devastated the field. The man whose name was engraved on the trophy, Hale Irwin, merely survived.

And barely survived. Irwin shot a 73 on the final day, yet somehow that was enough. In his decade and a half on the tour, the quiet, bespectacled man from St. Louis has proved that he plays difficult courses well, with two U.S. Open victories, plus a dozen more wins on courses such as Harbour Town, Riviera, Butler National, and Pinehurst Number Two. He is not a birdie machine, despite his course record, 62, at Pinehurst. No, Irwin prefers a course where par or its equivalent is a winner.

Par would have been golden at Winged Foot in 1974, but no one came close, not even Irwin, who struggled throughout the final round. By the time Hale made the turn into the last nine, it had become a battle for survival between him and twenty-three-year-old Forrest Fezler. Irwin bogeyed ten, then got it back with a birdie on eleven, and held on with par at twelve. There was another bogey at thirteen, and once again a comeback birdie at fourteen. But then it began to look as if the wheels had come off—bogeys at fifteen and sixteen. Some say the key to his victory came at seventeen when, after hitting an errant drive and a weak recovery shot, he lofted a one-hundred-yard pitch to within ten feet of the cup and sank the putt for a scrambling par four. This was a crucial save, to be sure, but it nonetheless left him at the back edge of one of the toughest finishing holes in the world.

Number eighteen at Winged Foot's West Course is the ultimate example of architect A. W. Tillinghast's calculated deviltry. A narrow right-to-left dogleg, it penalizes errant drives, and rewards only the long accurate ball. The approach shot must be played into a narrow, undulating plateau green guarded by several cavernous bunkers. The player who fails to hit this green in two may not hit it in three either. For the Open, the championship tee had been pushed twenty yards back into a hollow of elms, stretching the par-four hole to 448 yards. As a result, number eighteen had proved to be the third hardest hole in the Championship.

As Irwin pulled the driver from his bag, he knew he was either in first place alone or tied, but he knew no

more than that. Certainly, he had to make at least a par on eighteen.

He began the hole perfectly, with a long drive that split the fairway. Then, standing nearly 215 yards from the green, he selected a two-iron and addressed the most important shot of his life. As he stood to the ball, he knew the shot would have to do several things. It would have to be powerful and high; it would have to be straight; and it would have to stop quickly after it reached the slippery, fiercely-sloping green.

The result was all of that, an absolutely majestic stroke. The ball covered the pin from the moment it left the club, landed on the putting surface, hopped a couple of times, and then settled twenty feet in back of the pin. From there Irwin took two putts for par and a 72-hole total of 287. This was seven over par, but it was good enough for a two-stroke victory.

Playing the Long-Irons

For the average player, the most feared clubs in the bag are the one-, two-, and three-irons. Indeed, very few golfers even carry a one-iron, and in recent years the two- and three-irons have become more and more scarce as the lofted woods have grown in popularity. Granted, the five-, six- and seven-woods are easy to hit and offer many advantages, but no matter how many good shots you hit with them, they will never give the visceral pleasure of a well-stung, straight-as-a-string two-iron.

Besides, the long-irons are vital weapons if you play a lot in windy conditions. They're also helpful when you need to keep the ball low, under a tree or other obstacle. And, when struck properly, they offer better accuracy and more roll than the lofted woods. Furthermore, if you think about it, the long-irons are not as forbidding as they seem. Even the two-iron has more loft than the three-wood, and all of the irons are shorter than all of the woods, so they should be easier, not harder, to play.

Most problems with hitting the long-irons stem from one of three basic errors: improper grip, improper balance or improper timing.

The game's greatest long-iron players—Jones, Nelson, Snead, Hogan, Palmer, Nicklaus, Irwin—have all shared one asset: a consistent grip. Without a correct hold on the club, all shots are difficult and long-iron shots are virtually impossible.

In a proper grip, the club lies diagonally across the left hand, starting at the bottom joint of the index finger and extending so that the butt hits the palm just below the little finger. The hand wraps around the club so that the thumb points directly down the center of the shaft. You grip with the right hand as if you were shaking hands with the club, closing the hand over the left hand so that the left thumb nestles in the channel between the butt and the thumb of the right hand.

The way you link your hands— overlap, interlock or ten-finger grip—is up to you. Large-handed people gen-

The long irons must be hit with a sweeping impact to the back of the ball.

erally prefer the overlap or Vardon grip, in which the little finger of the right hand overlaps the index finger of the left. Small-handed people, including Jack Nicklaus, find more control in the interlock, where the little finger and index finger intertwine. And some very good golfers, Art Wall and Bob Rosburg among them, play with the ten-finger grip, with no linkage of the hands.

Whatever grip you use, be sure you hold the club so that no fewer than two and not more than three knuckles of the left hand are visible when you sole the club squarely behind the ball. Also, be sure that the "V's" formed between the thumb and forefinger of each hand are parallel and point at your right shoulder. This will give you a firm, well-knitted grip that will not let you down, on long-irons or any other shots.

You can insure good balance by taking a shoulder-width stance with your weight evenly distributed between both feet. The ball should be played a little more forward than usual, somewhere between the left heel and instep, to encourage a slightly more sweeping swing than you would use on a middle- or short-iron. Although the key with those clubs is to

The short irons are struck with a descending blow to the bottom of the ball.

hit down crisply on the ball, this downward blow is not as important with the long-irons. Instead, you want more of a sweeping impact, so you should position the ball at the point where your swing reaches the bottom of its arc— for most people that point is opposite the left instep. Your alignment should be square, or parallel to the target line. From this position, you should be able to swing in balance, assuming you keep the length and speed of the swing under control.

The swing itself must be firm but never hard, full but never long. Above all it must be a *swing* and not a hit. A firm swing begins with a one-piece takeaway from the ball. "One piece" means that your hands, wrists and arms all move straight back from the ball together and as one solid unit. At the same time, your lower body begins to move with a kicking in of the left knee. This one-piece takeaway helps you maintain balance, protects against flippiness in the wrists and starts the swing on a low, wide, sweeping arc— the same motion you want when you swing the club back through the ball.

There should be no wrist break at all until your hands swing past your right thigh. At that point, you should begin to make your backswing coil, striving to make as full a turn as possible. Once again, all the great long-iron players, from Jones to Nicklaus, have been able to generate a full, ninety-degree-plus turn of the shoul-

The key to solid shots on the long irons is a smooth, well-controlled swing, moving from a one-piece takeaway to a full, unhurried backswing coil, into a well-balanced impact.

ders, with the club shaft at least parallel to the ground at the top and the back facing the target. Not many golfers can do this, but the closer you can get the better. The key is to reach this position in a smooth and unhurried manner, and to come out of it in the same way. It is at this crucial top-of-swing position that most long-iron shots come a cropper, as the "hit impulse" takes over and the golfer casts at the ball with his hands and arms. One of the best ways to initiate the downswing is to move your lower body laterally toward the target. You can accomplish this by sliding your left knee to the left just as you reach the top of the swing. That one movement will automatically cause the right knee to follow, and it will also cause a downward pull on the hands. As a result, the clubhead will be pulled down and through the ball rather than being thrown at it. You will swing through the ball rather than hit at it. In the words of the great instructor Ernest Jones, "the ball will be merely an incident in the path of your swing."

It's almost impossible to think of anything between the top of the backswing and impact, but if you can keep one idea in mind, make it this: "Hit past your chin." Wait for your right shoulder to pass under your chin before you raise your head and body into the finish. This thought will help you to stay down and through the shot and will all but eliminate the chance of topping the ball.

So check your grip and take a firmly balanced, square stance with the ball off your left instep. Make a one-piece takeaway into a full, unhurried backswing. Then let your left knee trigger the forward swing, staying down and through the shot until your right shoulder passes under your chin. It may seem like a lot to remember, but if you take it all to the practice tee a couple of times, it will become second nature, and you'll never have to agonize over the long irons again.

IF YOU DARE: THE WINDCHEATER

Perhaps the most aggressive use of the long-irons is the low draw into the wind. When played properly, this shot will stay down much better than any wood shot, and it can roll as far as a driver. To hit it, play the ball just in back of the left heel in your square stance. Grip down an inch or so on the club. Then, after taking your grip, rotate your hands clockwise so that you open up the club a few degrees. This move will set your hands and arms in a slightly open position and will encourage you to make a slightly in-to-out swing, just enough for a gentle draw.

JERRY PATE
at the U.S. Open

The iron from rough

It may have been golf's finest shot under maximum pressure. Certainly no one will argue that when Jerry Pate struck the ball 194 yards, out of heavy grass and over water to within three feet of the eighteenth pin at the Atlanta Athletic Club, he played a supremely masterful stroke under the most demanding conditions imaginable.

Pate also claimed victory in the 1976 U.S. Open with that shot. It was the first professional triumph for the twenty-two-year-old former U.S. Amateur champion, and with it he became the first player since Jack Nicklaus in 1962 to win both the Open and Amateur crowns.

Moments before Pate played his shot, three other golfers had a chance to win, and all stood on that eighteenth hole. On the green were Tom Weiskopf and Al Geiberger, both with lengthy putts for pars and four-day totals of 279, five under par. Two hundred yards in back of them, in the right rough of the 446-yard dogleg, was John Mahaffey, also at five under.

The hapless Mahaffey had been a sentimental favorite, having lost the Open a year earlier at Medinah in a playoff to Lou Graham. This year he had led the second and third rounds, once by as many as six shots, and had held the advantage for most of Sunday as well. But his normally steady game began to unravel at sixteen, where he missed the fairway, and seventeen, where he three-putted. Pate, paired with Mahaffey, had played steadily all day, especially over the closing holes. A birdie on fifteen moved him to within a stroke of Mahaffey, and pars on sixteen and seventeen gave him a one-shot edge as Mahaffey bogeyed both holes.

The drama at eighteen heightened as Geiberger drilled in his twenty-footer and then Weiskopf followed with a seven-footer. Now Pate would have to par the hole to win; Mahaffey would need a birdie.

No, Mahaffey would need a miracle. Two hundred and twenty yards from the green, and in a very grassy lie, he had little choice but to use his three-wood and swing with all his might. But, as the year before, it was not to be. The ball splashed into the center of the pond.

Pate was several yards in front of Mahaffey, and his lie was considerably better. Still, when members of his gallery saw him select a five-iron, they began to murmur. He had almost 200 yards to the flag, and the pin was cut near the water. Although pros are strong hitters, very few of them ever use a five-iron from that distance. It normally calls for a hard four or a smooth three.

But Pate realized he was not in a normal situation. First, his adrenaline was pumping hard; he was hitting the ball longer than he had been even an hour before. More importantly, he knew his lightly grassy lie would produce a "flyer," that peculiarly unpredictable shot that darts from the clubface and flies ten to twenty percent farther than a shot from the fairway. Finally, he knew the ball would not be likely to "bite" on the green. Flyers have relatively little backspin, and they tend to take a bounce or two and roll a bit before coming to rest. So Pate did not aim his shot straight at the pin—the landing area was too small, with water in front and sand in back. Instead, he pointed his stance toward the longer, wider right side of the green.

After working his feet into a comfortable stance, he stretched into a wide, powerful backswing, then flashed through the ball into the high, stylish, uninhibited finish which is his trademark. As expected, the ball took off fast and soared high into the Georgia sky. But it was not the shot he had wanted—he had pulled it left, exactly in the direction of the flagstick. Now he would have to get lucky—the ball would have to clear the water yet sit

quickly enough to stay out of the sand.

For a second, there was silence in the cathedral of the green. Then the roar went up as twenty thousand people saw the ball stab the green and stop barely three feet from the hole.

As he approached his putt, the dazed rookie asked then USGA President Harry Easterly, "I don't have to sink this to win, do I?" "No, you don't," replied Easterly.

But sink it he did, to take the Open by two shots. The following week he proved he was no fluke, shooting a final round 63 to win the Canadian Open by four shots from Jack Nicklaus. In those two weeks a star was born.

The Flyer

It's convenient to think of rough lies as being divided into three categories: flyers, floater and flickers. The flyer is the most common, and is the one Jerry Pate conquered. In this lie the ball sits roughly half-covered by the grass, neither perched nor buried. The lie is called a flyer because of its tendency to produce that extra high, extra long shot. You get the added height and distance because blades of grass come between your clubface and the ball, inhibiting your ability to impart backspin. In exchange for this extra distance you will get less accuracy than from the fairway.

Two rules govern club selection on flyers. First, take one club less than you would for the same distance from a fairway lie, to compensate for the flyer effect. Secondly, on thickish lies, don't use any iron less lofted than a five. Once you get into the four-, three- and two-irons, it becomes difficult to swing the light head of the club cleanly through the grass for solid impact. So when you *must* have distance from grassy lies, go with a lofted wood—ideally a five- or six-wood—which has a smooth, heavy head that glides through the thick grass and into the back of the ball.

The most important principle in hitting iron shots from rough is to minimize contact between the clubface and the grass. You do this by making an upright swing, where the club rises quickly on the way back then descends sharply back to the ball.

The major adjustment involves ball position, which should be slightly farther back than for a fairway shot, roughly off your left heel.

Use a slightly open alignment, with your toe line, knees, hips and shoulders pointing slightly to the left of your target. This will set you up for the upright swing. Don't make any grip changes, except to hold onto the club a little more firmly than you would on a fairway shot. The firmer grip is necessary because the heavy grass tends to wrap around the hosel of the club, causing the face to twist into a closed position just prior to impact.

Most of your weight should be on your left side—about sixty percent left, forty percent right—on middle-iron shots; seventy/thirty on short-irons.

Before hitting the ball, take a couple of quick practice swings to test the grass. You may learn something about the lie—maybe the grass is tougher or easier to swing through than you thought. If it's tougher, you'll want to be sure to keep that left hand grip extra-firm. If it's easier, you may want to use a shorter club.

Make a slow, deliberate takeaway from the ball, and then a firm downswing. Firm, not hard. Lead the club through with your hands, and be sure to swing all the way up into your follow-through. Don't let the club die in the weeds.

The Floater

When you find your ball nestled deep in thick rough, the best shot you can hope to produce is a floater. The thick grass will slow your club to the point that you'll barely be able to extricate the ball. And whereas the flyer takes off like a rocket, the floater ascends more in the manner of a blimp.

Obviously, floater lies demand a lofted club, anything from the eight-iron to the sand-wedge, with the pitching-wedge being the best all-around selection. Unless you're within close range, forget about going for the green. In bad rough, your first objective should be to get the ball back to the fairway, then worry about the flag.

Generally you use the same setup as for a flyer, but, to give yourself an even more vertical swing, take a wide open stance, with the toe line, knees, hips, and shoulders all pointing several feet left of target. You will want an extra firm grip in your left hand, and, to further offset the club-twisting effect of the grass, you might want to open the face of the club (point it a few degrees to the right) at address. That way, if the club does close, it will close to a square position at impact. An alternative is to keep the face square at address but aim a few feet right of target, so that, in effect, you pull the ball at the target.

Make a smooth backswing, and don't take the club back more than three-quarter length. Then, on the way down, pull through impact firmly with your left hand. That will help you make a downward chop to the ball which will lift it up and out of the rhubarb. Once again: Be sure to finish the shot with a full follow-through.

The Flicker

Ficker lies look easy but are not. You have a flicker if your ball appears

The three rough lies:

the flyer, *playable with several irons and woods;*

the floater, *usually requiring a blast-out with a wedge;*

and the flicker, *permitting woods or even a driver.*

to be sitting up perfectly when it's actually perched on a tuft of rough. Such a lie invites you to belt the ball 200 yards. But you'll never *belt* it 200—you have to flick it.

The flick swing is different from all other kinds of rough-lie swings. Instead of gouging the ball out with a steep downward chop, you clip it off the grass with a horizontal sweeping action, much as you would a drive or fairway-wood shot.

It may look like a lucky break, but the flicker lie can be as treacherous as any rough lie you ever encounter. More than any other shot from high grass, it demands care and precision. First, take a close look at the lie to determine the exact level at which the ball is perched. In doing this, tread softly; if you should dislodge the ball it will cost you a penalty stroke.

Once you've determined the height of the ball, choose the appropriate club. In this case, you may indeed use a long-iron or a wood—in some instances it's actually advisable to use these less lofted clubs. Figure on getting the same distance you would from the fairway.

Begin by holding the clubhead to the ball at the ball's height, whether an inch or a foot off the ground. This may mean that you'll have to choke down a bit on the club. Again, be careful during the address that you don't topple the ball from its perch.

Your one object on the flicker is to take the club back low and wide to promote a flat, sweeping arc through impact. To encourage this, play the ball in its normal position in your stance, or perhaps even an inch more forward, and shade your weight slightly to your right side. Also, be sure that at address your left shoulder is higher than your right. Then just make a low, wide, firm-wristed takeaway and think of sweeping the ball off its perch, just as you would a teeshot. Swing easily and not too far back, and extend your arms through impact out toward the target.

IF YOU DARE: FINE POINTS ON ROUGH

Although we've divided rough lies into three categories, the truth is no two situations are exactly alike. Each lie in heavy grass is influenced not only by the position of the ball but by the condition of the grass, the direction of growth of the grass, and the species of grass, all of which add or decrease resistance to the clubhead.

More resistance
• Wet grass
• Grass growing against shot
• Bermuda grass

Less resistance
• Dry, parched grass
• Grass growing with the shot
• Bent or rye grass

When there is more resistance, you'll want to play the ball well back near your right heel, open your stance and, on the floater lie, go to an open-bladed sand-wedge. You'll also want to swing down more firmly than usual. When there is less resistance, expect the flyer to become a superflyer and the floater to fly almost normally. You may want to take two clubs less than you would from the fairway, e.g., a six-iron instead of a four.

BOBBY JONES
at the British Open

Fairway bunkers

Much golf literature of the last half century has focused on the year 1930, the final episode in the brief, brilliant career of Bobby Jones. Winning the Open and Amateur championships of America and Great Britain in a span of six months, Jones performed the Grand Slam, a feat that has never been equaled, seldom even approached. But in the fascination with that one year, golf historians have sometimes overlooked Jones' *other* awesome season, a season that may have been the necessary prelude to the Slam.

The year was 1926, when Jones got to the fifth round of the British Amateur, finished second in the U.S. Amateur, and won the Open Championships of both Great Britain and the United States.

In the first leg of that journey, the British Open, Jones looked as if nothing would ever stop him. At Sunningdale near London he led all qualifiers, shooting rounds of 68 and 66, with the latter eighteen hailed at the time as the finest round of tournament golf ever recorded in Britain. In the opening two rounds of the championship proper, at Royal Lytham and St. Annes, Bobby cooled slightly, but his pair of 72's nonetheless staked him to a two-shot lead over Al Watrous, with whom he was paired for the final 36 holes.

Watrous, a young pro from Grand Rapids, Michigan, who has been called the greatest golfer never to win a major championship, played hard in the morning round of that final day, posting a 69 which took him from two strokes in back to two in front. Through most of the final eighteen, Watrous held his edge, but he tightened in the stretch, three-putting fourteen and fifteen to allow Jones to draw even. Pars on sixteen kept the match deadlocked. Then, at the penultimate hole, it was Jones who cracked. His teeshot on the 411-yard par four drew left too much and too soon, coming to rest in an area of unraked sand just at the corner of the dogleg. Watrous drove safely down the right side of the fairway, then knocked a long-iron onto the front of the green.

Jones was a shot and a half from the green, yet needed to get home in one.

In his book, *Down the Fairway*, he described the predicament.

• • •

The only way I could get a look at the green, and what lay between it and my ball, was to walk far out to the right, nearly across the fairway. I did this. The prospect was not precisely encouraging. I had to hit a shot with a carry of close to 175 yards, and hit it on a good line, and stop the ball very promptly when it reached the green —if it reached the green. This, off dry sand, though the ball luckily lay clean, was a stiff assignment. You know, an eighth of an inch too deep with your blade off dry sand, and the shot expires right in front of your eyes. And if your blade is a thought too high—I will dismiss this harrowing reflection.

• • •

Jones selected a four-iron, and with that lazily graceful swing, swept into the ball, stinging it cleanly from the sand. It shot out over the dunes and upward into the wind, arching just over the greenside bunker and onto the green, where it settled well inside the ball of Watrous.

Completely unnerved, Watrous again three-putted. Jones got his par, then parred eighteen as Watrous bogeyed in. The victory was by two shots, but truly, the day was decided by a single magnificent stroke.

From a Fairway Bunker

Most short bunker shots may look difficult but actually are relatively simple to play. The long shot from a fairway bunker, however, is just as tough as it looks. Few situations demand a more precisely executed swing. Mis-

play the long fairway bunker shot, even just a little, and you will pay dearly.

For this reason, most golfers should not try to play from fairway traps with any club less lofted than a four-iron. Woods are rarely advisable except in the most favorable situations, where you have little or no lip to clear and a perfectly clean and level lie.

Since the goal on this shot is to make absolutely solid impact, all effort should be geared toward control rather than power. Your object is to strike the ball first, with no sand coming between the clubface and the ball. To do this you must use a swing that promotes a relatively horizontal or sweeping angle of attack, where the clubface swings directly into the back of the ball and makes contact at the very bottom of the swing arc. This type of impact is, of course, in direct contrast to the markedly downward hit that is neces-

Take a wide stance, and dig your feet well into the sand, for maximum balance.

sary on greenside sand shots. But around the green the object is to hit all sand and no ball. In the fairway bunker you want all ball and no sand —at least, not until after impact.

You can assure the sweeping impact by making a couple of changes in your set-up. First, instead of using the open stance demanded for shorter sand shots, set up squarely with the toe line, knees, hips and shoulders all aligned parallel to the target line. Second, spread your feet well apart, as much as a foot wider than your normal stance. This will widen your swing arc, thereby widening the bottom of your swing and promoting a sweeping impact, while also helping you to maintain balance and control. You will further enhance your control by digging your feet firmly into the sand. Just be sure that you grip down on the club at least as much as the depth you dig into the sand, because otherwise you'll risk hitting the shot fat and leaving the ball in the bunker.

Since you must grip down on the club and must also play for control rather than power, select at least one club more than you would for a fairway shot of the same distance. Two clubs more is even wiser.

The position of the ball is very important. It should be off your left heel. This will mean that you will catch the ball as your club is just at the bottom of its arc, or perhaps just beginning to come up. In any case, by keeping the ball forward, you will eliminate the chance of hitting behind it, taking too much sand and leaving the ball in the bunker.

As for the swing itself, just think of two words: low and slow. Keep the club low to the ground in your takeaway (just above the sand—but don't touch the sand unless you want a two-stroke penalty). If you take it back long

and low, you will also approach the ball in that way, and that's exactly what you must do when playing from a fairway bunker.

You also want to keep things as slow and deliberate as possible both during the backswing and in the first move into impact. Don't hit from the top—don't throw the club at the ball with your hands. Just swing the club; let it do all the work. If you have set up correctly, the club should simply act as a pendulum. Let it sweep forward and through the ball. The less you "try" on this shot, the more satisfying the results will be.

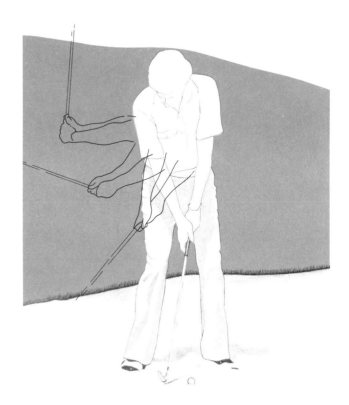

Keep the backswing slow and deliberate. The less you "try" the more you succeed.

IF YOU DARE: SLICE IT OUT

Sometimes the lip of the bunker is too high or the lie is not clean enough to permit a normal shot. In many of these situations an intentional slice can save you. By cutting across the back of the wall with an open clubface you'll increase the initial trajectory of the shot and will also dig a bit more into the sand to help raise the ball.

Take two clubs more than you would from the fairway, and address the ball from an open stance with a slightly open clubface. Also aim several yards left of your target. Otherwise, play the shot as described above. (If the ball is down a bit in the sand, play it back an inch more in your stance—just back of the left heel.) If all goes well, you'll get a high, soft, sharply-fading ball that will sit quickly after it hits the green.

BYRON NELSON
at the Crosby

The intentional hook

Of the hundreds of thousands of golf holes in the world, none is more famous—or more formidable—than the sixteenth at Cypress Point. A 233-yard par-three, stretched across the crashing surf of California's Monterey Bay, it is the breathtaking epitome of heroic golf course architecture. And yet, in the minds of many, this majestic hole is merely a brassy prelude to the elegant par four which follows it.

The seventeenth at Cypress is worshipped by some, reviled by others, but respected by all. In the four decades

since Dr. Alister Mackenzie designed the course, this masterful dogleg has beckoned the best and worst from those who have played it. And it was here, in 1951, that Byron Nelson took the biggest gamble of his career.

The Bing Crosby National Pro—Am that year signaled a surprise return to the tour for Nelson, who had formally retired in 1946, one year after his incredible string of eleven consecutive victories. Coaxed by Crosby, Nelson unsheathed his game for one more tournament. And he played as if he had never left.

For most of the first two rounds Lord Byron was flawless, displaying the powerful drives and surgically accurate approach shots for which he was famous. When he came to the seventeenth tee he was leading the tournament—but about to put himself in jail.

The tee at number seventeen sits just above and in back of the sixteenth green, and, as at sixteen, the teeshot must cross 200 yards of the Pacific. The hole angles right, skirting the craggy ocean cliffs all the way to the green. Thus, on the teeshot one may cut off as much or as little water as one dares. To complicate matters, a copse of large, gnarly cypress trees sits dead in the center of the landing area, about 250 yards out.

Off the tee one has three options: one, take an iron and play well short of the cypress trees, then play a two- or three-iron over them to the green; two, drive past and to the left of the cypress trees, thereby increasing the dogleg but allowing an unimpeded middle-iron approach to the green; or, three, gamble with a teeshot to the right of the trees, cutting off lots of ocean and leaving a short-iron to the green. The one place *not* to be, other than the Pacific, is directly in back of those cypress trees.

And that of course is where Nelson hit his ball. He tried to play safely to the left, but pushed the ball slightly, so that it finished smack in the shade of the trees. As he approached his ball, he resigned himself to his plight—he would play a short pitch over the trees and then another pitch to the green, in hope of a one-putt par.

Then he got another idea.

"A strong wind was blowing in off the Pacific that day," recalls Nelson, "and I knew if I could hit a huge hook out over the water, the gale might just turn it back hard enough and fast enough for the ball to catch the green. It was a bigger risk than I had ever taken, but I'd been playing so well that day that I thought I could bring it off.

"I took a three-iron, addressed the ball, and aimed myself out at the cliffs. When my playing partner, Eddie Lowery, saw what I was doing, he started running toward me, yelling for me to stop my insanity.

"But it was too late. By the time I heard his voice the ball was in the air, heading out toward the surf. It hung out there—twenty-five yards out—for what seemed like a full minute. Then, just as I had planned, it drew sharply back in. It must have hooked forty yards or so before it stopped about twelve feet from the pin.

"By that time Lowery was shouting, 'You stupid fool, if I had reached you in time I would never have let you hit that shot—it could have cost you the tournament.' He was right—if the shot hadn't come off, I would have taken at least a six. But as it worked out I parred the hole and went on to win by one shot."

It was the last of Nelson's fifty-four career victories.

The Controlled Hook

Of all the shots in golf, the big, controlled hook is probably the hardest to hit. Comparatively few golfers have the setup and swing which naturally encourage a right-to-left shot. Most players are some variation of fader/ slicer, with an open alignment, an out-to-in swing, and a host of attendant idiosyncrasies which combine to make the hook shot nearly impossible.

But even the game's best players have trouble with the hook. Granted, most of the pros are able to summon the right-to-left ball when the situation dictates, but only twenty or so players can consistently control that kind of shot on drives and approaches. The reason is that the hook is a far "hotter" shot than the slice or straight ball. A hook has less backspin and more sidespin than a slice, and as a result it flies lower and curves more violently than does a slice. As Lee Trevino once said, "You can talk to a fade, but a hook won't listen."

Fortunately, however, there are three good ways of playing a hook. Although each method is suited to a different level of golfer, a high-handicapper can attempt both the basic and intermediate methods, and any player in the ten to fifteen handi-cap range can try the advanced as well as intermediate and basic techniques.

Basic Method

This is the most mechanical of the options, and consists largely of an al-teration in the address position. First, square the clubface to the target line. Then, take a markedly closed stance, so that your toeline, knees, hips and shoulders all point at least thirty de-grees to the right of the target line. Be especially sure that your shoulders are closed—they may *feel* closed, but if you're naturally a fade/slice hitter, you probably play habitually from an open shoulder alignment, and when you think you have closed your shoulders for this shot, you may have actually brought them only into a square posi-tion. So, when you practice this shot for the first time, ask a friend to tell you where your shoulders are aligned. The ball should be positioned off your left instep, and you should feel as if about sixty percent of your weight is on your right side.

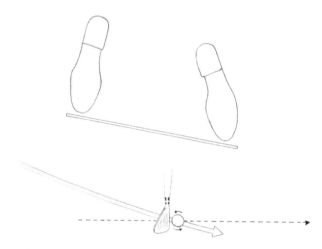

A closed address position encourages the in-to-out impact that leads to a hook.

This address position will set you up for the necessary in-to-out swing path, and you need not now make any changes in your swing. If you have ad-dressed the ball correctly the shot will come off naturally. The more hook you need, the more closed your address po-sition should be.

If you find the change in setup does not give you enough right-to-left flight, make a change in your grip as well. Simply rotate both hands a quar-ter-turn clockwise on the grip. Assum-ing your grip is the standard one, this new position will have the "V's" formed by your thumbs and forefingers pointing just outside your right shoulder. The new grip will help promote the inside takeaway, flatter swing plane and in-to-out impact that you need.

Intermediate Method

If you have a reasonably well-grooved, orthodox swing, and can hit the ball at least 200 yards off the tee, you can try a more sophisticated method of hooking the ball.

This method is best described as "handsy" and, while it has the advantage of being easy to "program," it has the disadvantage of being difficult to regulate. It's simple to hit a hook—even a big hook—with this method, but hard for most players to hit a controlled hook with it. Much practice will be necessary.

To hit a handsy hook, set the clubface square and then align your

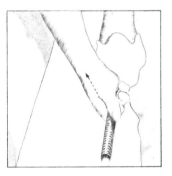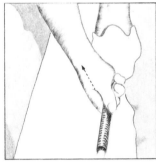

Strengthen your grip by rotating both hands so that the V's point at your right shoulder.

body ten to twenty degrees closed to your target line, slightly less closed than you would if you were using the basic method. From this square address, make just one alteration, which is the key to the handsy hook. Rotate the clubface to an open position, by rolling your wrists open. The toe of the club should rotate several degrees to

the right, and you should be able to see one to two more knuckles of your left hand than you normally do. (*Note:* This is not a regripping of the club, but simply a rotating of the hands. When you initially set the club square to the ball, you should have your grip in place and you should not move it when you fan the clubface open.)

By rotating the clubface to an open position, you simultaneously lower your right arm and shoulder slightly into a position that will encourage a markedly inside takeaway and a return to the ball from inside to out. But the secret is just to let the swing happen, and not to think about what you've set up at address. Trust the hands method, and it will work. The more hook you want, the more you should open the clubface.

Advanced Method

A good player should have a solid swing and a thorough understanding of golf-shot ballistics. He should also be good enough an athlete to make his body execute the moves that will force the ball to "cooperate." In essence, he should be able to summon the *feel* of a hook swing, and execute that swing almost totally by feel. This feel can come intuitively, as it does with many fine strikers of the ball, or it can come as the result of long practice using the other two methods described here. In either case, once the feel is there, it needs only to be programmed, or triggered, which is the crux of the advanced method.

The first step is to use lots of visualization. "See" yourself hitting the ideal shot, and see your body making the strong in-to-out move through impact with the legs driving and the hands swishing from inside to out in the hitting area. Remember the best good player you should be able to do this.

Even if you have trouble with the visualization, you should be able to program the "feel" hook simply by the way you approach the shot. If you're a true golfer, you probably take your address position by walking up from behind and inside the ball. Exaggerate this, and "come into the ball," club in hand, the way you want to come into it in your swing, sharply from the inside.

Later in your address pattern, make your waggles so that the clubhead flashes markedly to the inside, and start to feel the hook swing in your arms and shoulders as you do so. If possible, continue to visualize that perfect swing and shot you hit. Finally, when you make your swing, concentrate on moving your body the way you want to make the ball move; sweep into the ball with the feeling that you are moving everything in a counterclockwise circle, turning into the ball with your body, yet sending it outward with the club. At impact you should feel your shoulders, hips and arms all closing like a big door as your clubface pushes outward through the ball.

A good player can summon a hook simply by visualizing the proper swing and flight path.

hook shot you ever hit and try to remember and visualize the swing you used on that occasion. If you're truly a

IF YOU DARE: PLAY THE PERCENTAGES

A subtle key to success with the intentional hook is to know the lies and conditions that favor or discourage it. You might be surprised to learn, for instance, that a slightly sandy lie can be good. If the sand gets between your clubface and the ball it can increase the friction and help you put spin on the ball. As another example, a tailwind, helpful on a straight ball, will be harmful when you are trying to hit a hook—it will tend to straighten it out. Certain clubs are easier to hook than others, too. Here's a quick list to help guide you:

Helps a Hook	*Inhibits a Hook*
Four-wood, five-wood, six-wood	Driver, two-wood, three-wood

Four-iron, five-iron, six-iron	One-iron, two-iron, three-iron, seven-iron, eight-iron, nine-iron Pitching & sand wedges
Ball up on grass	Ball down in grass, heavy rough, wet grass
Uphill lie, sidehill lie with ball above feet	Downhill lie, sidehill lie with ball below feet
Headwind, right-to-left wind	Tailwind, left-to-right wind
Sandy turf	Bunker lie

NANCY LOPEZ-MELTON
at the Bent Tree Classic

The intentional slice

Ask a hundred professional golfers to name the most satisfying moment of their careers, and ninety of them will have the same reply: Victory Number One. Nothing is sweeter than breaking the ice.

For Nancy Lopez-Melton, the first win came more quickly than it does for most players, but it did not come without a struggle. She had been on the LPGA Tour for nine weeks when she found herself in the thick of the race for the 1978 Bent Tree Classic in Sarasota, Florida.

"In the last round I was even with Jo Ann Washam as we came to the fourteenth hole, a par four," she says. "I had been playing well all day—all week, in fact—but on that teeshot I lost the rhythm and I pulled the shot badly. The ball flew into the left rough, dead behind a tall palm tree.

"There was no way I could play a straight shot to the green—I was absolutely stymied. Since I was to the left of the fairway, the logical shot was to start the ball right of the tree and hook it back to the green. But I have never had confidence in my ability to control a right-to-left shot. My natural shot is just the opposite, a fade. The trouble was that to hit a fade—in this case, a slice—I'd have to start the ball straight at a creek which ran up the left side of the fairway all the way to the green. If, for some reason, I failed to put enough slice spin on the ball, I'd be in that creek and out of the tournament."

Nancy's predicament was complicated by the fact that she was in heavy grass, which inhibited her ability to spin the ball. Nonetheless, she chose a six-iron and readied herself for the most important shot of her young career.

First, there was the setting of the stance, her body aimed directly at the very creek she hoped to avoid. Then, the familiar Lopez "ignition," a slow raising upward of the hands prior to the takeaway. Next, the arms pulled back around, then sharply upward, stretching to the top of the swing. From there, the legs flashed and the

61

body uncoiled in a powerfully synchronized release.

The ball took off high and fast—and straight at the water. Then, as if on command, it began to curve gently back. For a long moment it looked as if it would not curve back enough. But then, at the last second, it dived sharply onto the left edge of the green. From there the rookie took two putts to save her par. Another par at sixteen kept her tied with Washam, and on seventeen she sank a fifteen-foot birdie putt to take a one-stroke lead which proved to be her margin of victory.

Nancy won the next event as well, and the following week she lost a play-off to finish second. In the month of May she won three consecutive events, then two more back-to-back in June. By the end of her first season she was not only Rookie-of-the-Year, but Player-of-the-Year as well, with a new money-winning record of $189,813. At Bent Tree, Nancy had launched one of the most spectacular seasons any golfer—male or female, rookie or veteran—had ever produced.

The Intentional Slice

A sliced shot curves from left to right because the ball spins that way, in a clockwise direction. The ball spins that way because at impact you strike it a glancing blow with your clubface open to (facing to the right of) the path of your swing. The more open that clubface is in relation to the swing path, the bigger curve the ball will make. It's as simple as that, which explains, in part, why so many golfers slice.

You can create a slice almost entirely at address. The key is the open stance, with the toe line, the knees, hips and shoulders all parallel and pointing left of the target. For a slight fade you can align as little as ten or

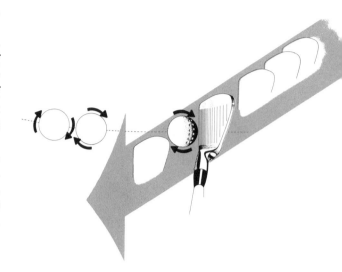

In a slice impact, the clubface is open to the swing path, imparting clockwise spin.

fifteen feet left of the target; for a roundhouse slice, aim at least twenty yards left.

Don't worry too much about ball position. If you keep the ball off your left heel you should be fine. If anything, experiment by moving the ball back a little, because if the ball gets too far forward in the stance you will contact it as the clubface is beginning to close, causing a pulled or pull-hooked shot.

At address, the clubface should be square to your intended target, not open. Note, however, that when it is square to the target line, it *is* open to (pointing to the right of) your alignment. You must understand this point. It can be confusing, because the term "open," when used in reference to clubface alignment, means (for right-handed players) "pointing to the right," but when used in reference to body alignment means "pointing to the left." In any case, if you align your stance left and your clubface at the target, you will be in the proper position for a left-to-right shot.

From there it is simply a matter of making a good swing at the ball. Don't make any major changes—just swing smoothly.

Now, you may find that, even with the open stance and square clubface, you knock the ball directly to the left, with not the slightest hint of a slice. When that happens you have probably allowed the clubface to close through impact, putting it on the same line as your open stance, causing you to hit the ball straight left. The shot is called a pull, and you can correct it, as noted above, by experimenting with ball position and also by firming up the grip pressure in your left hand. Gripping the club tightly with the left hand makes it harder for the right hand to roll over and close the clubface, or "release" into the ball at impact. Instead,

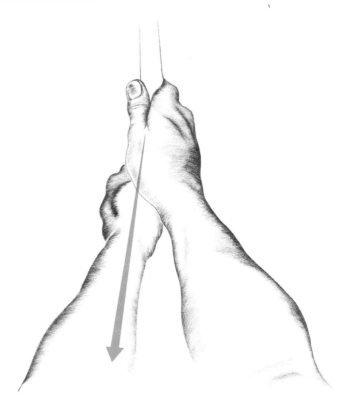

In a weakened slice grip, the V's of both hands point at your left eye.

your left hand stays firm, leading the right hand through. This is essentially the same move Lee Trevino uses to hit his super-accurate fade. Lee holds the clubface on line well through the impact area by not permitting the right hand to roll over the left. You can work toward the same move simply by firming up that left hand grip.

If a rearward ball position and a firmer left hand grip pressure still don't give you a big enough slice, then "weaken" your grip a little, rotating both hands to the left on the club until the "V's" formed by your thumbs and forefingers point to your left eye. It will feel strange and unnatural, but, like the firmer grip pressure, it will work to inhibit the rollover of the right hand and will encourage the out-to-in swing

At address, your body is aligned well left but the clubface points directly at the target.

necessary for this shot. A final word: Since a left-to-right shot normally saps you of distance, to fade the ball take one club more than you would for a straight shot, and two clubs more if you're playing a big slice.

An important but often overlooked aspect of playing any shot as demanding as the intentional slice is the mental side. You must first plan the shot correctly, visualizing the ideal path and trajectory. To give yourself confidence, try to recall a similar shot you played well.

Once you've chosen a club, take a couple of quick practice swings, striving for the same feeling you had when you hit a particularly good intentional slice. Alternatively, imagine Trevino's swing—the open alignment, the hands holding firm through impact, the legs and hips shifting laterally toward the target. As you swing, try to put that type of motion into your body. Don't make any conscious "moves." Simply try to imitate the whole picture of the Trevino swing—you'll be surprised how effective this can be.

IF YOU DARE: KNOW YOUR LIMITS

As with the intentional hook, certain clubs, lies and course conditions favor the intentional slice or fade, and it's extremely important to know what they are:

Helping	*Inhibiting*
Driver, two-wood, three-wood	four-wood, five-wood, six-wood
one-, two-, three-irons	seven-, eight-, nine-irons, wedges
Hardpan, tight lie	Rough, thick fairway lie
Downhill lie	Uphill lie
Sidehill lie, ball below feet	Sidehill lie, ball above feet
Headwind, left-to-right wind	Tailwind, right-to-left wind
Clean lie on sand	Any other lie in sand
Dry grass	Wet grass

GARY PLAYER
at the PGA

The high shot

Ben Hogan glumly surveyed the 76 on his scorecard and proclaimed, "This course is a monster."

The occasion was round one of the 1951 U.S. Open. The setting was suburban Birmingham, Michigan. The course, the monster, was Oakland Hills. Designed by Donald Ross and modernized by Robert Trent Jones,

the South Course at Oakland Hills is without question one of the hardest par-seventies in the world. In the last century it has hosted a total of six major championships—four U.S. Opens and two PGA's—yet few men have truly tamed it. One who did was Hogan, who, in the final round in 1951, reversed the numbers of his

opening score and "brought this monster to its knees" with a 67 that gave him the third of his four Open titles. Another was Gary Player, the determined little South African who clinched the 1972 PGA Championship when, on the seventieth hole, he played one of the most electrifying recovery shots in the history of professional golf.

Player had begun the final round with a three-stroke lead, but faltered early, bogeying three of the first four holes. After that the chase was on, with a dozen men in close pursuit. Player struggled through the next dozen holes, twice missing short putts that could have put him back in command. When he came to the sixteenth tee he was tied for the lead with Jim Jamieson, a burly journeyman pro who had never quite broken through to the top echelon.

On a course famed for its awesome par fours, the sixteenth may be the most awesome of all. A 408-yard dogleg right, it sweeps around a large, menacing pond that has ended the title hopes of many a competitor. The hole is not overly long, but it calls for two well-struck, well-placed shots.

Player's drive was neither well-struck nor well-placed. A horrible, twisting slice, it sailed straight for the pond but fell short, lodging in the deep, damp rough, dead behind one of the largest weeping willow trees in Michigan. It left him with a near-impossible assignment for his approach shot. He would have to hit the ball high enough to clear the willow tree, yet long enough to reach the green, 150 liquid yards away.

"Normally I hit a seven-iron 150 yards," Player later remarked. But he knew a seven-iron would never lift the ball over the tree. Neither would an eight-iron. He would have to hit a nine-iron, and hit it harder than he ever had before.

"I had to gamble," he said. "I could not see the flag from where I was, so I aimed for a seat stick I spied between the branches." The little man pumped every ounce of his power into the swing, slashing down and through in an explosion of grass and turf. The ball tore out of the wet turf, skimmed the very top of the tree and burst upward into the gray sky. It hung there for seemingly endless seconds, as Player and everyone else wondered whether it would clear the pond.

Then the ball stabbed into the green, four feet from the hole. Moments later Player sank the putt for a birdie. It gave him a lead of two shots, his eventual victory margin.

Hitting for Maximum Height

For many players, the most difficult aspect of golf is getting the ball into the air—high into the air—with consistency. The problem is particularly prevalent in the long irons, which produce more tops and fat shots than proper impacts. For this reason, most golf clubs of the last decade have been designed with extra weight in the sole area, the theory being that this weight will help get the club down and under the ball, forcing it upward more easily.

These sole-weighted clubs can probably help you, but the best way to get extra height on your shots is to make a couple of changes in your setup and swing. The mechanical adjustments recommended here will help you, whether you want to arm yourself with the short-iron shot Gary Player hit or simply increase the height of your three-iron shots.

Height results from a combination of two things: the loft on the club and the angle at which you contact the ball.

Alignment should be slightly open, and most of your weight should be on your right side.

hands will hang in back of the ball—in fact, they'll be in back of the clubface as well—which will increase the built-in loft on whatever club you're using. If, for example, your nine-iron has a built-in loft of forty-eight degrees, you can increase that to an effective loft of fifty degrees or more by setting up with the ball in the forward position.

The other major adjustment is in the distribution of your weight. You should lean slightly to the right so that most of your weight is on that side. This will help you to keep your body and hands in back of the ball throughout the swing, thus maintaining the extra loft you have created on the clubface. It will also help you swing in a way that will bring your club into impact at the very bottom of the ball so that you can loft it easily upward.

Both can be established in your address position.

Your alignment should be slightly open, with your toe line, knees, hips and shoulders all pointed a few degrees left of your intended target. Be aware that on longer shots this set-up will also cause you to slice the ball, and in those instances you should allow for the left-to-right drift.

The ball should be played one to two inches forward of its normal position in your stance, which for most people means off the left instep. Your

To hit the ball high, finish high, with your hands reaching for the sky.

The final adjustment is to grip the club lightly to promote a long, free-flowing swing that will allow your hands to release the club smoothly through impact, a prime requisite for the high shot.

Once you've set up correctly there is little to fear. Just concentrate on making a full, controlled swing. At impact, you should feel as if your body is well behind the ball and your arms and hands are whipping through and quickly upward. The light grip pressure will help you to get that feeling. Strive for a high, majestic finish, hands pointing skyward. And just be sure that your head and body don't raise up *too* quickly—that could spoil an otherwise perfect swing.

Perhaps the most important advice in playing the high shot is to know your limitations. First, don't try to clear a tree that you *know* you cannot clear, even with your best shot. And if you find yourself in a situation where you need a nine-iron to clear the tree but a five-iron to reach the green, don't tell yourself you can compromise by hitting a high, hard seven-iron. Go with the nine-iron and get back into play, then shoot for the green. Finally, know which lies are "friendly" to the high shot and which are not. Fluffy lies in the fairway or in light rough are ideal, as they make it easy for you to get the club under the ball. Conversely, the high shot is difficult from tight lies, such as hardpan, sand and close-clipped fairways.

IF YOU DARE: REACH FOR THE SKY

If you're sure of your ability to make solid contact no matter what kind of swing you have to use, try this more aggressive technique; it may help you to clear the unclearable tree. First, increase the "openness" of your stance by pointing your body several yards left of your intended target. Second, address the ball with a wide-open clubface, so that the blade of the club faces well to the right of the target line and also lays back a bit, increasing its effective loft even more than usual. Do everything else just as recommended above (ball forward, weight on the right side, light grip pressure). During the swing, strive for the feeling of cutting across the ball, as on an intentional slice. Swing the club back to the outside, and, as you come into impact, keep the wrists firm; don't let your right hand pass your left until after impact. Then go ahead into the high finish. What you'll get is a blocked-slice type of impact, but with the clubface open and the ball forward it won't slice too much. Instead, it will be a high shot. Practice this one a few times before you try it in actual play. Once you learn it, you'll find that it will help you hit the ball higher, even with the long-irons and from tight lies.

PATTY BERG
at the Titleholders

The low shot

She had been there before. When Patty Berg teed it up for the stretch run of the 1957 Titleholders Championship in Augusta, Georgia, it was old hat. No matter that she was two shots behind the leader, Anne Quast. Berg had won the Titleholders six times. And she was determined to go all out for number seven.

A par at the first hole, a birdie on two and then, on the short par-five third, on in two and down in one for an eagle. Three holes under her belt, and she was three under par. After another par on the fourth she came to the most vulnerable hole on the course.

"Number five was a short par five, a dogleg right," recalls Berg, "just the type of hole that tempts you to cut the corner. I knew that, with a strong, fading teeshot, I could easily reach the green in two and pick up another birdie, maybe even another eagle. But I also knew that if I cut the shot too much, I'd be in the worst kind of jail."

The right side of the fairway was lined with tall trees, and beyond the trees the ground dropped off 100 feet into a ravine from which there was almost no return. "On a couple of occasions I had drifted down that slope," admits Berg, "and I had never escaped with less than a seven.

"On that day, though, I told myself I was playing too well to worry about negative results. But I guess I wasn't playing well enough. Two seconds after impact I knew I was cooked. The ball never even flirted with the fairway. Into the trees and down the hill it went."

When Berg finally climbed down to her ball she realized her options were severely limited. Clearly, she couldn't play a shot for the green—the treeline was impossibly high and dense. For the same reason she couldn't hit a lofted shot out of the ravine. "I saw that my only escape route was the 'low road.' With a bit of luck I could smack the ball up the slope and under the lowest hanging branches of the trees. It was a longshot, but it was my only shot," she says.

Berg picked out the largest opening in the trees, reached for her four-iron and pelted sharply into the back of the ball. It raced up the hill, bounced once, and skittered under the trees and into the center of the fairway. From there she knocked a three-iron to the edge of the green, chipped up stiff and sank the putt for a working woman's par. Berg finished the nine with 33, returned in 36, and won the tournament by three shots.

"I played steadily the last thirteen holes," she says, "but the key to my victory was that shot from the ravine. It kept a good round—and my confidence—alive." Together with her five other victories in 1957, the win made Berg the LPGA's leading money winner for the third time in four years. Perhaps more significantly, her seventh triumph in the Titleholders established a record (for multiple victories in a single event) which has never been equaled.

Hitting Low Shots

For many players the hardest aspect of golf is getting the ball into the air with adequate trajectory. Since that is the case, hitting low shots should be relatively easy. However, shots such as the one played by Patty Berg require more than a little finesse.

First, the shot must be carefully planned. Be sure, at the outset, that your lie permits a low shot. If you're in heavy rough you will have trouble keeping the ball down. In order to get out of tall grass, you must normally use a downward-driving swing, which creates height. If you try to sweep the ball low out of the rough, the clubface can get slowed down or caught, and you can easily leave the ball in the grass. The ideal lie for a low shot is hardpan where there is no grass near the ball at all, so that you can make clean, solid contact with the back of the ball. However, you should also be able to play a low shot from the fairway

and even from light rough.

Once you're sure your lie permits a low shot, try to visualize the ideal path and trajectory. This will help with club selection. If the imaginary shot seems to call for a five-iron, play it safe and take a four.

Whatever club you choose, grip down on it a little for better control. Play the ball back in your square stance, at least two inches in back of where it normally would be—for most golfers this means about midway in the stance. This will leave your hands in front of the ball, and most of your weight on the left side. This ball position also will cause you to "hood" the clubface slightly (lean the top of it toward your target), thereby reducing its effective loft. Finally, this address position will encourage you to keep the clubhead low as it goes through the ball.

To start the swing, firm up your grip and make a long, low one-piece takeaway, stretching your arms outward as you move the club straight back from the ball. If you take the club back low to the ground, you will return it to the ball in the same way, and that will give you a low trajectory.

On longer shots, don't be afraid to make a conscious transfer of your weight from left to right as you take the club back. This will give you the low, wide swing arc you need. Just be sure that the transfer does not become a "sway." The firm grip will help you limit the length of your backswing to about three-quarters the normal turn insuring that you keep your swing under control and make a clean impact.

The follow-through on this shot also is shorter than normal, and also is low, with the hands and club pointing outward at the target. Remember, to hit low, finish low.

Grip down a bit, and play the ball well back in your square stance.

Stay low throughout the shot, especially as you move into the follow-through.

IF YOU DARE: THE PUTTER POP

In selecting a club for low shots, too many people overlook an obvious choice, the putter. Certainly, when you must hit the ball extremely low (but not too far) the putter is the ideal choice. It has only four degrees of loft, whereas the next least-lofted club, the driver, has ten to twelve degrees. Secondly, the putter is the shortest club in the bag, and therefore the easiest to feel and control. And it can be extremely useful in a situation where you might never expect to use it—from heavy rough around the green. When you don't have to flip the ball over a bunker or other obstacle, you can often be most effective by "popping" the ball out of the heavy grass with a putter. Just open the stance slightly, play the ball back as you would for a low shot, and, using a wristy swing, pop the putter down on the back of the ball. The ball will take one big hop out of the grass and then scoot into a long run. In many cases, popping with the putter is wiser than trying to chip or pitch the ball from unpredictable high grass.

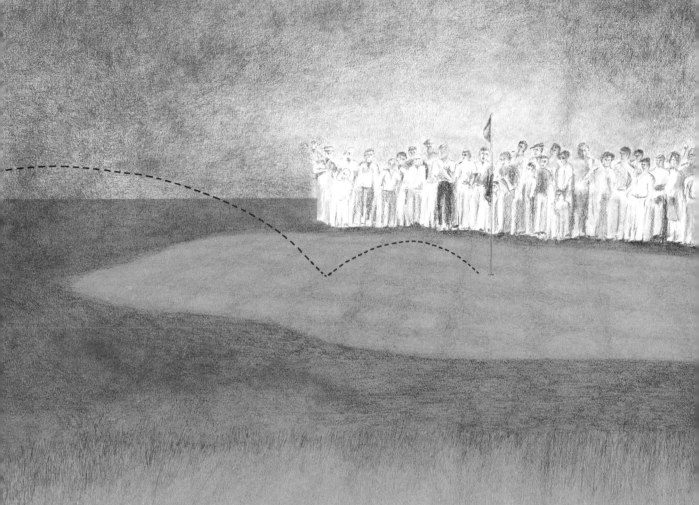

PETER THOMSON
at the British Open

The long explosion shot

Birkdale, 1954. As twenty-four-year-old Peter Thomson addressed the most important shot of his life, an old saying floated through his mind: "Sydney or the bush."

"It goes back to the Australian sheep shearers," Thomson says. "Once a month they were paid, and that eve-ning they started drinking and playing cards. Gradually the stakes would swell, until at some point late in the game one of the shearers would an-nounce, 'All right, it's Sydney or the bush,' tossing his entire bankroll into the pot. If he won the hand he'd take off for Sydney and live like a king until the money ran out. If he lost, it was back into the bush country."

In the two Opens prior to 1954 Thomson had come painfully close to "Sydney," finishing second to Ben Hogan at Carnoustie in 1953 and to Bobby Locke at Royal Lytham in 1952. Now he had the lead, late in the final round, but he was being chased by the same Locke, by Spaniard Tony Cerda and by Welshman Dai Rees, each of them a single stroke back.

And Thomson was in trouble. His second shot on the sixteenth hole, then a 510-yard par five, had dived into a deep bunker twenty-five yards short of the green.

"My heart was in my mouth when I saw that lie," he recalls. "Whatever reputation I have was built not on my skill in overcoming trouble as much as on my ability to avoid it altogether. In fact, thinking back over my years as a professional, I can't recall too many fine recovery shots or daring gambles. But this one was enough for an entire career.

"The ball had pelted into the front bank of the bunker but had bounced out of its imprint so that it was lying relatively cleanly. Still, it was on such a steep slope that, when I addressed it, my left foot was nearly a foot higher than my right. To make matters worse, there was another huge bunker directly between me and the green, so that if I caught the shot a bit too heavily I was dead. This was normally a birdie hole, but now I was just hoping to get my third shot into a position from which I could get down in two for a par five."

He did even better. Using an old MacGregor Double Duty sand-wedge, Thomson hit a sort of "hybrid" shot. Neither a pitch nor an explosion, more of a "splash," it landed on the front of the green, took a couple of hops and

settled three inches from the cup. Birdie four.

Thomson parred the last two holes and won the championship by one stroke. It was his first victory in the British Open, but hardly his last. Over the next four years he won the title three times and finished second once. Then, in 1965, he returned to Birkdale for an incredible fifth British Open—only Harry Vardon, with six, has won more.

Two Ways to Play "The Hardest Shot"

Among amateurs and professionals alike, the long greenside bunker shot is regarded as the most difficult assignment in golf. Take too much sand and you leave the ball well short, usually in the same bunker. Take too little and you skull the shot into the face of the bunker or clean over the green and into a new predicament.

You will improve your ability to play long shots from bunkers if you learn the two alternative methods, which are matched to the two most common types of lies.

The Long Splash:

This is the shot that Peter Thomson played. You can use it only when you have a clean or almost clean lie, with the ball sitting on top of the sand or in only a small depression. With the splash you take a relatively shallow cut

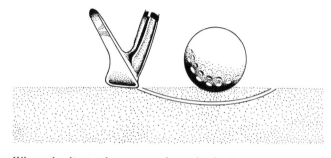

When the lie is clean, use the splash shot, taking a shallow cut of sand.

Use a low takeaway, with a slow, natural breaking of the wrists.

of sand and hit a rather high, quick-stopping shot; when played perfectly, the ball will even spin backward a bit on landing. This is also a good shot to play when you have to fly the ball a long way, as when another bunker or other obstacle prohibits you from bouncing or rolling it to the pin.

To play the splash shot, take a wide open stance with your toe line, knees, hips and shoulders aligned almost forty-five degrees left of your target, digging in deep with both feet for maximum balance. Keep the ball off your left instep so that your hands are slightly behind it and your weight is about sixty percent on your left side.

Hold the club so that it is slightly open (facing right of the target) and also lay it back so that its back side is nearly parallel with the sand. This will encourage the skimming type of im-pact you need, with the club slicing through a thin layer of the sand rather than digging deep into it.

Make a low takeaway with a slow, natural break of the wrists, and swing your hands back and up only to about shoulder height. Keep your eye fixed on a spot about two inches behind the ball and concentrate on entering the sand *shallowly* at the point. You want to penetrate no more than an inch under the surface. Swing through the ball fully—don't leave the club in the sand or your ball will stay there too. You can regulate the distance of this shot by in-creasing or decreasing the force of your swing. Generally, you should swing about twice as hard as you would on a pitch shot of equal length.

The Long Explosion:

When the ball is buried, or when you have a cuppy or fried egg lie, your only alternative is the explosion. Un-like the splash, which flies most of the way to the pin, the explosion floats out lazily, lands well short of the pin, and then rolls most of its way to the hole. This makes it a good choice when you have no obstructions between you and the pin, and can afford to play a more predictable, rolling shot.

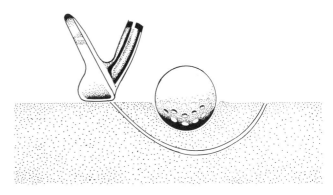

On heavy lies, explode the ball with a downward, knifing cut into the sand.

The objective on the explosion swing is to make a deep, knifing cut into the sand, to dig well down under the ball. To effect this type of impact you need a more vertical, downward swing than that used for the splash.

The explosion swing begins with a quick and marked cocking of the wrists.

Set up in the same open stance used for the splash, but this time position the ball farther back, off your left heel. Your clubface should be square to the target, and at least seventy-five percent of your weight should be on your left side.

On the backswing, make a quick wrist break so that you swing the club steeply upward. This will help to program the sharply descending blow you need on the downswing. The swing should be slow but firm, about three-quarter length, with a minimum of weight shift and almost no leg and body movement. On the downswing, lead the clubhead with the hands, and concentrate on digging down and through the ball. This time you want to dig at least three inches under the sand's surface. Once again, be sure to swing fully through the shot. The best way to regulate distance on the explosion is to vary the distance you hit behind the ball. The closer to the ball you penetrate the sand, the farther the shot will go. If you experiment with distances from one to four inches, you'll begin to develop some "touch" for this difficult shot.

IF YOU DARE: THE MID-IRON BLAST

When the lip of the trap is low and there's a long stretch of green between you and the pin, a six-iron may be a better explosion club than a wedge. Grip down two or three inches and play a standard explosion, digging into the sand two to three inches behind the ball. You'll get a mid-height explosion that will take one big bounce and then scoot into a long roll.

MICKEY WRIGHT
at the U.S. Women's Open

Uneven lies in sand

There was the pressure of the hometown crowd, of playing in front of her parents for the first time, of being number one, of being expected to win. And, ultimately, there was the pressure of the national championship—on the final day, on the final hole. It all came to bear on Mickey Wright in 1964.

For seven years she had dominated the women's tour. Five victories in 1958, five more the next year. Six in 1960. Then ten each in '61 and '62 before a record thirteen in '63. In the process she had won four LPGA Championships, three U.S. Opens, three leading money-winner crowns, and four Vare Trophies for lowest scoring average on the LPGA Tour. Not even Babe Zaharias had compiled such a record.

In 1964 Wright continued her reign, winning eight tournaments by mid-July. Only Ruth Jessen had challenged Mickey's supremacy, with six wins. On two occasions Wright and Jessen had tied in regulation play, but

Wright had won both playoffs. Now, at the San Diego Country Club, the two were battling again, and this time for the big one, the U.S. Open.

As Wright prepared to play her tee shot on the final hole she knew she needed a par to tie Jessen and force yet another playoff.

The drive was perfect, long and straight down the fairway of the 420-yard par four. All along the ropes friends and neighbors from Wright's native San Diego called out encouragement, while, near the green, her parents nervously awaited their daughter's final strokes.

"It was a long hole," recalls Wright, "the longest par four the USGA allowed for women, yet I remember telling myself I could get home with a well-hit 2-iron. Well, I guess I tried a little too hard, because I pushed that ball straight into the bunker guarding the right-hand side of the green."

When Wright reached the result of that shot she knew her problems had just begun. The ball was on the extreme right side of the bunker, on a severely downhill lie, and the pin was more than 100 feet away. "Fortunately, it was sitting pretty well," she says. "If it had been buried, it would have been all over. Still, I knew that with the uneven stance I'd have to make a near-perfect swing. A little too much sand and I'd leave the ball well short of the hole; too little and I'd skull it clear over the green, or, worse, into the face of the bunker for an instant double-bogey.

"I had been in several Opens and I'd had my share of pressure, but I remember thinking this was the most tension I'd ever felt. As I stepped up to that shot I just told myself, 'You can't mess up—not here, not this time.'

"The next thing I knew I was watching one of those explosions you dream about—a high, soft shot that rose up and over the lip of the trap, floated across the green and dropped down softly five feet under the hole."

It left her with an uphill, left-to-right breaking putt which she knocked straight into the cup. The next day she outplayed Jessen once again, 70 to 72, to win the last of her four Open championships, a record which stands to this day.

The Downhill Bunker Shot

The downhill sand shot is an easy shot to miss badly and a hard one to execute well.

Fortunately, the ball will seldom bury in a downhill lie. On the rare occasions when it does, the best advice is simply to "get out any way you can." Often this means blasting safely out sideways or even out the back of the bunker directly away from the hole. However, since this type of problem accounts for probably no more than ten percent of all downhill bunker lies, we'll concentrate on the more common

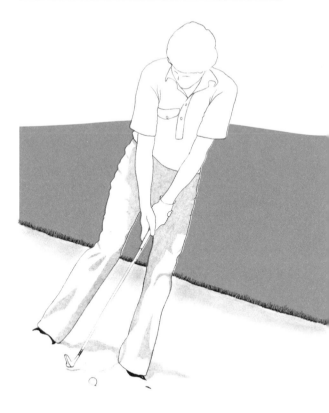

Your stance should parallel the slope, and the ball should be just back of the left heel.

situation—a good or moderately good lie, where the ball sits relatively cleanly on the slope, as it did for Mickey Wright.

As with all downhill lies, your stance should be more or less parallel to the slope. In a bunker the best way to achieve this is to dig in a little more deeply with the left foot than with the right, to kick in the right knee slightly, and to incline the shoulders a bit so that the right is above the left. You can check your setup by looking at your belt—if it's roughly parallel to the slope you're in good position.

Also, as is the case with all downhill lies, your shot will tend to have a lower-than-normal trajectory, so allow for that in advance by opening the face of your sand-wedge a degree or two. Be aware, however, that by opening the face you will also increase the tendency of the club to "bounce" off the sand at impact. To counteract that, you will have to make a concentrated effort to hit down and under the ball.

You can encourage the downward blow by positioning yourself so that the ball is between your left heel and the middle of your open stance. The backswing should be smooth, but the downswing should be very firm and should be initiated by the hands, which should work actively through this shot, to make the club approach the ball on an angle parallel with the slope.

If you normally penetrate the sand two inches behind the ball, you should enter three to four inches behind it for this shot. The reason is that the sand is deeper in back of the ball than in front, so the club will slide through too quickly and produce too low a shot unless you explode from a large cushion in back of the ball.

On an uphill lie, use an open stance and keep your hands even with the ball at address.

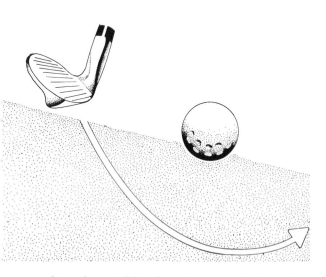

On a downhill bunket shot, your club must enter the sand three or four inches behind the ball.

Remember to swing down firmly; when you're hitting four inches behind the ball you can afford to put some extra power into the blow. Besides, the worst mistake you can make is to leave the ball in the sand, so use plenty of force, and, most important of all, *follow through.* Just after impact, both the ball and your hands should be moving at the hole, but at almost perpendicular angles.

The Uphill Bunker Shot

While not as difficult as the downhill bunker shot, the uphill shot is tricky and is frequently left short of the hole.

All uphill shots tend to fly higher and shorter than shots from level lies, so you must keep this in mind and expect to swing somewhat harder than normal. Pretend the pin is ten feet farther away than it actually is.

Once again, it's important to align your body parallel to the slope. On an uphill lie you can do so by setting your weight back on your right side and flexing your left knee slightly. However, be aware that this will also inhibit your ability to make a natural follow-through, so you'll have to make a special effort to swing through fully on this shot. Most golfers fail to do so, and that's why they leave the ball short.

Ball position should be off the left heel, the stance should be open and the hands should be just about even with the ball, with the clubface square to the target.

Make the same swing as on any explosion shot, but with one adjustment. Hit only an inch to an inch and a half behind the ball. With an uphill lie, the sand is deeper in front of the ball than behind it and thus you'll naturally be digging up a big, deep cushion, so you

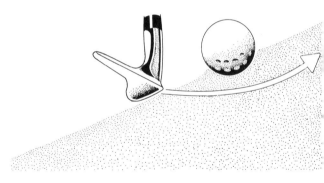

You won't need to take too much sand—hit only an inch behind the ball.

don't need to take a lot of sand behind the ball.

Expect a high, floating shot without much roll. On a forty-foot bunker shot from an uphill lie, you can count on carrying the ball thirty to thirty-five feet and rolling it the last yard or two. From the downhill lie, just the opposite will be true—a flight of five to ten feet and thirty feet of roll.

IF YOU DARE: THE THUMP SHOT

When you're plugged near the front lip of a bunker with just ten feet to the pin, it can seem like an impossible situation, but actually it's one of the easiest of all sand shots. The answer is simply to "thump" the ball out. Play the ball in the center of your wide-open stance and shade 75% of your weight on your left side. Then, *close* the face of your sand-wedge—yes, *close* it. This will help you dig down and under the ball. Play a firm explosion shot, but instead of following through, simply thump the club down forcefully into the sand about two inches in back of the ball. The ball will pop up softly, flop down on the front of the green and trickle toward the hole. The harder you thump into the sand, the higher and farther the ball will fly.

SAM SNEAD
at the British Open

The cut shot from sand

Sam Snead hadn't planned to go to St. Andrews in 1946. Hogan wasn't going. Neither was Nelson. And besides, the British Open was hardly a major championship. Not in 1946.

But still, it was a national championship, and that is why, at the last minute, Snead booked passage to Scotland. For a decade he had been one of the very best players in the world, winning more than forty professional titles. And yet he had never captured the most prestigious prize of them all—the United States Open Championship. Several times it had eluded him, most painfully at the Spring Mill Course of the Philadelphia Country Club in 1939. Needing only a par five on the final hole to win, Snead pushed his second shot into a bunker 100 yards short of the green, took two shots to get out, another to get to the green and three more to reach the cup for a disastrous eight, which left him in a tie for fifth place.

So it was with a sense of determination that Snead sailed for the birthplace of golf.

And, as was the case with so many great players before and after him, Snead was initially perplexed at how such an unkempt and randomly plotted string of holes could be regarded as one of the world's great championship tests. But after a week of practice he was as comfortable among the heather and pot bunkers of the Home of Golf as if they were the pines and hollows of his native Virginia.

He opened the tournament with a 71 and duplicated that score a day later to place two strokes behind leader Henry Cotton. On the final day inclement weather unraveled Cotton, among others, and Snead's uneventful morning round of 74 staked him to a tie for the lead with Johnny Bulla, Dai Rees, and the South African tiger, Bobby Locke. Snead had struck the ball well all week, and he knew that if he could play his own game and avoid major mistakes for one more round he would win the championship.

In the afternoon, a raw wind blew in from the North Sea, making St. Andrews' outgoing nine play even longer and harder than a few hours earlier. After the first four holes Snead was three over, three-putting twice in that stretch. And now he faced the big hole —number five.

Now, in the course of almost every major championship the contenders seem always to be called upon to play at least one highly daring or dangerous shot and often in the final round. But it is almost inconceivable that a champion golfer would face three such shots *in a single hole.* Yet that is exactly what befell Sam Snead on the fifth at St. Andrews.

From the beginning this treacherous 567-yard hole, the first of only two par fives at St. Andrews, had Snead on the ropes. Driving into the strong wind, he hurried his release slightly and hooked the ball wildly into the cavernous and aptly-named Hell Bunker. With over 350 yards left to play, every inch of it into the wind, Snead knew he needed a good recovery shot, despite the high lip on the bunker. He chose a three-iron, opened the blade slightly, and cut it up and out of the sand. But the wind accentuated the left-to-right spin on the ball and dashed it back across the fairway into the right rough where it lodged in the center of a thick clump of gorse. To make matters worse, the gorse had snared the ball on the bounce so that it now perched fully a foot off the ground. And, to complicate matters still further, the gusty wind was blowing the ball back and forth like a pendulum.

"I'll never forget trying to address that shot," says Snead. "I just stood there, moving my club back and forth,

back and forth, trying to get in rhythm with the sway of the bush. Finally I decided to take a swipe at it. I'll tell you what, I made one of the best swings of my life. It was a long, low six-iron, and it went a lot farther than I thought it would. In fact, it went clear into 'The Eyes.' "

"The Eyes" is another of St. Andrews' feared hazards—a pair of large, deep bunkers lying about 140 yards short of the fifth green. For more than 500 years these bunkers have snatched the second shots of golfers, turning pars into disasters. And Snead had hit into "The Eyes" on not his second shot but his third.

Suddenly it all looked just too familiar: leading a national championship in the final round; in the bunker of a par-five hole in three shots; lots of golf still to play.

The fact was that Snead faced a far more difficult shot now than he had had seven years earlier at Spring Hill. "When I bent down to address the ball, the lip of the bunker was higher than my hat. I had a pretty good lie, but what I had to do was make that ball climb almost straight up. What's more, I had to hit the ball about 150 yards if I wanted to get it to the flag. I remember thinking, 'You don't have a club in your bag that will do the job. You need an eight-iron to reach the pin, but the loft of the eight won't get you over the lip. A wedge will get you out, but not on.'

"Finally, I decided to take a nine-iron and try to hit it as high and as hard as I knew how. I remember opening my stance wider than I ever had, laying back the clubface, and swinging the club as if it was a hatchet. On the way down I slipped the clubface under the ball with a quick flicking motion.

"It worked. I picked the ball clean yet caught it solid. It shaved the grass on the lip of the bunker and climbed up toward the green, where it stopped about twenty feet from the hole. From there I took two putts for the most welcome six of my life."

A bogey six. Not a par, but not an eight either. The scenic series of shots, particularly that final one, steadied Snead with the confidence that he had weathered the worst. From that point on he played himself to a four-shot victory in the only major national championship he was ever to win.

The Cut Shot From Sand

The bunkers on most American golf courses are not nearly as treacherous as "The Eyes" at St. Andrews, and when a deep bunker does exist it is nearly always next to the green, not 140 yards up the fairway. Thus you'll rarely have to consider using an eight- or nine-iron, as Snead did. Most of your cut shots from sand should be played with the wedge—the pitching-wedge, not the sand-wedge.

The key on this shot is to slide the clubface cleanly under the ball. The sand-wedge, with its broad, heavy flange, cannot slide easily under anything. When Gene Sarazen invented this club back in 1932, he intended it as an explosion club, to dig down under the ball and then bounce back up through the sand. But on a cut shot you don't want either to dig or bounce, so it's wise to stick with the less broad-soled pitching wedge.

When you face a situation similar to the one that confronted Snead, all of your effort should be geared to one goal: height. You must make the ball climb quickly.

Address the ball with a wide-open stance, with your knees, hips and shoulders all aligned thirty degrees left of your target. This will set you up for the necessary upright takeaway and severely out-to-in impact, where the club cuts sharply across the ball imparting lots of backspin and sidespin.

Ball position is extremely important. Whereas in most sand shots you play the ball near the center of your stance, for the cut shot the ball should be farther forward, just off the left heel. This should put your hands about even with the ball and the club in a position that allows you to use its maximum loft.

The stance is wide open, and your pitching wedge should be open, as well.

In an extreme situation, such as the one Snead faced, you might want to move the ball even farther forward in the stance, so that your hands at address are actually in back of the ball. This has the effect of "laying back" the clubface, with the back of the club nearly parallel to the ground. But this is risky, for two reasons. First, if you aren't careful you can lay it back so far that it actually touches the sand at address, which will cost you a two-stroke penalty in stroke-play or loss of the hole in a match. Secondly, when the ball is too far forward and the clubface is laid back too much, you risk the chance of "bellying" the ball—hitting it with the leading edge of the club instead of with the clubface—and skulling it straight into the side of the bunker.

A safer way to add a few more degrees of loft at address is to open the clubface slightly, pointing it a few degrees right of your target line. In fact, when you use the wide-open stance it's very wise to open the clubface as well. By aiming the clubface to the right a bit you compensate for the markedly out-to-in swing which will direct the ball slightly to the left.

To develop that swing, work on making a quick pick-up of the club with your wrists, just as you take it

The key to the swing is the quick pick-up of the club.

back from the ball. This will get the club on an upright plane as quickly as possible. On the downswing think only of sliding the club under the ball. Try to forget about the sand, and, whatever you do, don't try to "help" the ball out of the bunker. If you've set up correctly and made the wristy pick-up, you won't need any special moves. Just think of slipping the club under the ball.

This is an easy shot to miss, either by hitting it too thin or too fat, but generally the thin shot will hurt you far more than the fat. If you take a little too much sand you'll probably get just as much backspin as if you hit it clean, but if you hit the ball a little thin, even a dimple thin, you may not get it out of the sand. So be certain you get *under* the ball. The way to ensure this is to have a good firm footing in the sand, and to keep your knees flexed throughout the swing. Picture your finish, with the knee-flex still present. That will help you avoid the sudden upward-jerking movements associated with "help-the-ball-up" anxiety.

On longish cuts from sand, you'll have to swing a bit harder, as Snead did. The ball will fly so high you will need power to get distance. And on all cut shots you can expect a certain amount of left-to-right drift, as well as a kick to the right when the ball hits the green. So for pinpoint accuracy, align that open stance and clubface just a little left of your ultimate target.

IF YOU DARE: TEST YOURSELF

Perhaps the toughest thing about hitting a cut shot from sand is deciding whether the shot is indeed possible—whether the quick-climbing escape is within the combined capabilities of you and your club.

Some of these shots are clearly playable while others are obviously impossible, but in doubtful cases you should be able to make an educated guess. And the best way to educate yourself is with a badminton net or a clothesline. Take your pitching wedge and a couple of dozen balls out in your yard and hit cut shots over the net or line. Start several feet back; then, as you begin to master the shot, see how close you can get and still make the ball climb up and over the net or rope. After a while you'll have a good idea of what you can and can't do with the ball. That knowledge will help you make the right decision whenever you face a tough cut-shot situation.

WALTER HAGEN
at the British Open

The chip from sand

In the long history of championship golf, surely no one ever played a greater number of brilliant shots in do-or-die situations than the legendary Walter Hagen. In golf, as in life, Hagen took the scenic route. While his opponents coaxed the ball cautiously from tee to green, The Haig went his own way, hooking it here, slicing it there, exploding from sand, slashing from rough, and flicking from the edges of the green. And more often than not Hagen's way won.

Sir Walter knew better than most golfers the limits of his own ability. From the tee he was neither overly long nor overly straight, and from the fairway he could hit the ball thirty yards off line just as easily as he could hit the green. So he followed a philosophy that served him well. "In a given round of golf," he said, "I expect to hit at least five bad shots." And he really believed it, so that when he served up his first errant ball he didn't become angry or disgusted. After all, it meant he had only four mistakes left for the day.

Hagen also knew his strengths—trouble play, short shots, and putting. On a par four he believed that if he could stay within shouting distance of the hole in two shots, he would make his par. So when his ball drifted into trouble, Hagen retained the two psychological assets that most of us lose: self-control and confidence. Many who saw him play say that The Haig's most impressive shots were those played from "hopeless" situations.

It was this resourcefulness from trouble, plus a strong competitive drive, that enabled Hagen to win an incredible twenty-two straight head-to-head matches and four consecutive PGA Championships from 1924 to 1927. Time after time, when he appeared to be out of a hole, Hagen plucked the ball from near oblivion and deposited it next to the cup, unraveling his opponents and delighting his fans in the process. As Henry Longhurst wrote, "Hagen's game was fallible and impertinent, which endeared him to the common man."

There may or may not be truth to the story that Hagen liked to step to the first tee of a tournament and announce, "The Haig is here—who's playing for second?" But one thing is certain: Hagen never played for anything but first. That attitude was perhaps most clear on a summer morning in 1922, the final day of the British Open at Royal St. Georges, Sandwich, England. On that day Hagen announced that he was prepared to risk anything to win the championship, that he had no interest in finishing second or third.

Late that afternoon, he was forced to prove his words.

Having played sixty-three holes of the championship in 264 strokes, Hagen reckoned that if he could finish the incoming nine in even fours, he would win. All went according to plan until the fifteenth, a short par four, where his second shot drifted into a wide stretch of sand known as the Cross Bunker. The bunker was not too deep, and the ball sat cleanly on the hard-packed seaside sand. Still, he had a long way, perhaps 100 feet, to the pin. Hagen assessed his two options: He could take the safe route and explode the ball out, or he could play a chip shot—a far more risky stroke.

As he mulled the decision, Hagen determined that if he tried to explode the ball, he would have to hit a high, heavy shot that would run out of steam well before it reached the cup. It would probably mean two putts and a bogey —but a safe bogey.

If, on the other hand, he could flick a chip shot over the lip of the bunker, it could surely roll up to the pin for a one-putt par, thus saving the stroke he would otherwise have to shave on the extremely tough final three holes.

The second choice was tempting, but Hagen knew that the chip from sand was the most demanding short shot in the game. Even though he had a good lie and a relatively low lip to clear, the shot would be a stern test. If he were to catch the ball even the slightest bit thin or heavy, he would leave it in the face of the bunker, which would almost certainly cost him the championship.

Hagen studied the shot for a long time, and changed clubs several times, from the wedge to the seven-iron, the seven-iron to the wedge and then back to the seven-iron. Finally he hefted the seven and set his feet firmly for the gamble. With a short, controlled stroke he clipped the ball off the top of the sand. It barely cleared the lip of the bunker, then skipped forward, quickly catching the contour of the undulating green. The ball rolled on and on, and, when finally it stopped, the cup was less than one foot away.

Hagen got his par, made four on each of the final three holes and fulfilled his plan, winning the championship by a single shot. He thus became the first native-born American ever to win the British Open.

Years later Hagen called that little chip the greatest golf shot he had ever played.

Chipping from Sand

It was Hagen himself who first said, "The sand shot ought to be the easiest shot in golf—you don't even have to hit the ball." But that flippant philosophy doesn't apply to the chip shot from sand. In this situation, you must hit the ball, the whole ball and nothing but the ball. If you don't, you will cost yourself at least one shot and more likely two.

As with many trouble shots, it is most important to know the conditions that improve or lessen your chances of success. First, the lie: *Do not* try this shot unless the ball is sitting cleanly atop the sand. Second, the lip of the trap: If it is higher than two feet, *forget* about chipping. (Incidentally, if there is no lip at all, you should also forget chipping; the putter is what you should use, assuming the sand is firm.) That brings us to condition three, the sand: If it is wet and tightly packed, you will have an easier chip than if it is loose, dry and soft. Finally, consider the distance of the shot: If it is reasonably long, fine, but if you have less than twenty feet to cover, you probably won't be able to stop the ball close to the hole.

Regarding club selection, if you like to chip with one club all the time, go ahead and use it. It's important on this shot to have confidence, and your favorite club will give it to you. Of course, if your favorite club is less lofted than a seven-iron, you'll be flirting with danger if you try to fly over a two-foot lip. So be sure that you consider the trajectory of your normal chip before you go with Old Reliable.

If you vary your choice of club according to your distance from the edge of the green and the distance from the edge to the pin, then follow your normal rules, but with one adjustment. Hit one club less (more lofted) than you normally would. For instance, on shortish chips, play a pitching wedge instead of a nine-iron; on long, run-

Chip from sand only when the lie is good, the lip is low, and the distance is ample.

ning chips take an eight-iron instead of a seven. In all cases, never use anything less lofted than the seven, and never, *never* use your sand-wedge for this shot because that big heavy flange can belly the ball right into jail.

This shot is played similarly to a normal chip, but with a couple of variations. Set up in a well-open stance and play the ball fairly far back so that your right toe is pointing at the ball. This positioning will help you to contact the ball first, before touching the sand.

The stroke should be absolutely stiff-wristed; you should swing as if your hands, wrists and arms were all bound to the grip of the club in a plaster cast. By keeping everything stiff, you'll insure that the radius between your hands and the clubhead you set up at address will remain unchanged throughout the swing. That way the club cannot dig into the sand or flip upward and into the top of the ball as it might if you use a wristy motion.

The length of your backswing should relate to the length of the shot. Since you're not using wrist action, backswing length is the only safe way to control the distance. So take a short swing for a twenty-five-foot chip, a longer swing for a fifty-footer.

The only other fundamental on this shot is a mental one: "Don't get scared." Try to play the shot with confidence, as Hagen did. Keep your eyes locked on the ball and bring the club firmly down and through it. Don't try

Clean, crisp impact requires a stiff-wristed, controlled swing.

to lift the ball off the sand, and don't stop the club short. If you hit down crisply on the ball it will jump easily over the top of the bunker lip. Just try to pretend you're playing a routine chip shot from the fringe. The chip from the sand will never be routine, but a little practice can make it a very useful addition to your shotmaking arsenal.

IF YOU DARE: "SUCK-BACK" SHOTS

If you're willing to put in a few practice hours in a bunker, you can truly work magic with long chip shots and pitches from sand. You'll find that by taking an infinitesimal amount of sand on your pitches, you can impart much more backspin to the ball than from a fairway lie. The reason for this is that a thin layer of sand acts like sandpaper, increasing the friction and spin on the shot. With the correct hand action, you can

actually make a wedge shot suck back several feet, but that takes practice. Still, if you're willing to put in the time, you can do it. Experiment with the stiff-wristed swing on shorter pitches, then use a bit of wrist break on the longer shots. Experiment with varying degrees of the out-to-in "slice" swing. Experiment, finally, with the amount of sand you take. In this case, you *do* want to miss the ball—just by about a millimeter. The best club to use on these shots is your pitching wedge, with the blade opened slightly for extra height and backspin. Be prepared to hit your share of bellied shots and fluffs, but be prepared also to see some backspin action you never thought you could produce.

BABE ZAHARIAS
at the Texas Women's

Hardpan and muddy lies

Golf

In 1930, the year Bobby Jones won the Grand Slam, no one had heard of a fifteen-year-old girl named Mildred Didriksen. Two decades later, when the Associated Press named its Woman Athlete of the Half Century, Mildred "Babe" Didriksen Zaharias won in a landslide.

To this day she remains the greatest female athlete of all time—not just a fine golfer, but a superbly versatile performer who dominated every sport she tried. As a teenager in Texas, the tall, slender Babe outbatted her brothers in baseball, outran them in track, outkicked them in football and outshot them in basketball. In 1932 she qualified for the U.S. Olympic Team, won a gold medal in the hurdles and another in the javelin throw, where she set a new world record on her only toss.

A year later she was persuaded by sportswriter Grantland Rice to try golf. She took to it naturally, and, under the tutelage of Tommy Armour and Gene Sarazen, she quickly began to play well. By 1935 Babe had learned to hit the ball long and fairly straight, had begun to sink her share of putts and had become an adept sand player, using a wedge given to her by Sarazen. That year she entered her first tournament, the Texas Women's Closed Championship.

She qualified with a 76. Then, surprising everyone, she breezed through her preliminary matches and reached the finals against the veteran tournament competitor, Mrs. Dan Chandler. In that match Babe played steadily, and through the fourteenth hole found herself three up.

But her second shot on the par-five fifteenth rolled into a muddy rut, several yards short of the green. "I was scared to death of that shot," she said later, "but I remembered the sand-wedge Gene had given me and shown me how to use. It sure did come in handy."

With a large crowd surrounding her the Babe waded carefully into the mud, sand-wedge in hand. Then, using her powerful man-like swing,

103

she splashed downward into the ball. As she did so, she lost her balance and fell flat in the mud. She was still there when the ball rolled into the cup for an eagle three. The jubilant gallery surged toward her, lifted her on their shoulders and carried her all the way to the clubhouse.

It was Babe's first victory but hardly her last. For twenty years she dominated golf in a way no woman ever had before, winning more than fifty amateur and professional titles, including an incredible seventeen in a row in 1946. That streak included her first U.S. Open, a title she won twice more. A year later, she became the first American to win the British Women's Championship.

When the LPGA Tour first took shape in 1947, the Babe was its biggest drawing card, and she won the money title four years in a row. She was named woman athlete of the year five times. But of all her achievements, none stirred the hearts of the public as did her fight against cancer. In 1953 Babe underwent surgery, amid rumors she would never play golf again. But a year later she came back to win the U.S. Open, by a record twelve shots. She won four more tournaments that year, and two more in 1955 before the disease became so debilitating that even the Babe's courage and determination couldn't overcome it. In September 1956, she died.

Golf's Dirty Work

If you play on a reasonably well-conditioned golf course, you won't often have to deal with muddy or hardpan lies. But when you do encounter them you should know how to handle them; otherwise they can cost you a great many strokes.

Muddy lies, such as the one Babe Zaharias conquered, are the worst of all because they're so unpredictable. It's often hard to determine how soft the mud is and how deep it goes before hard ground is reached, and if you don't know those two things you can't play the shot with either confidence or accuracy.

In essence, the best way to play a muddy lie is to play it almost like a bunker shot—explode it. Although the Babe used a sand-wedge, a pitching-wedge is an easier and safer club for most golfers to use. Hit an inch or so behind the ball and come down sharply into the ground, splashing the ball out on a cushion of turf. The harder or more congealed the mud, the closer you should hit down in back of the ball.

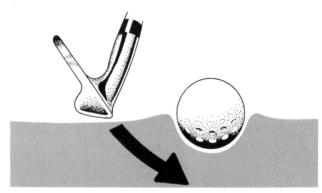

Mud is handled the same way as sand; hit an inch or two behind the ball.

On hardpan, your goal is to hit the ball first and hit it flush. You must not let your club touch down in back of the ball, because it will bounce off the hardpan into the ball, causing a skulled shot or worse, a whiff. So the idea is to pinch the ball between the clubface and the ground.

Set up in a square stance—toe line, knees, hips and shoulders all parallel to your target line. Also, widen your stance an inch or so to give your-

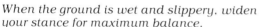

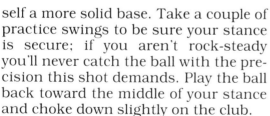

When the ground is wet and slippery, widen your stance for maximum balance.

Swing firmly, and pull through with the hands, just as on a bunker shot.

self a more solid base. Take a couple of practice swings to be sure your stance is secure; if you aren't rock-steady you'll never catch the ball with the precision this shot demands. Play the ball back toward the middle of your stance and choke down slightly on the club.

During your waggle and swing, keep your eyes on the front part of the ball. This will help insure that you meet the ball first, not the ground behind it. Your backswing should be as

steady as your stance, a smooth, firm-wristed, three-quarter swing. On the downswing, don't be afraid to swing firmly, but *do* lead through with the hands and keep your finish low, with the club pointing out toward your target.

The same general swing can be used for all lengths of shots, with club selection being the distance-controlling factor.

IF YOU DARE: AN EASY SHOT FROM HARD TURF

Ask the tour pros about hardpan and they'll tell you it's one of their favorite lies. The reason is that hardpan is a very good lie from which to hit a fading shot. With no grass intervening between the club and the ball, a good golfer can easily impart clockwise spin. In fact, you should have less difficulty hitting a controlled fade from hardpan than from the fairway. Actually, this is nothing more than a pinch shot in which you "quit." Play the shot exactly as described above, but, as you come into impact, hold your wrists stiff; in other words, don't "release." End the swing as soon after impact as you can. The result will be a low, fading ball that bounces to the right after it lands, but comes to rest relatively quickly. If you want more bend, simply open your stance slightly to promote a more out-to-in swing. For a high, fading shot, open the blade and play the ball slightly forward. Just be sure to block-out that wrist release at impact.

LEE TREVINO
at the British Open

The aggressive chip

"It was a no-brainer, an absolute no-brainer," says Lee Trevino of the shot that brought him victory in the 1972 British Open at Muirfield, the home of the Honourable Company of Edinburgh Golfers.

All week long Trevino had been the beneficiary of a large helping of dumb luck, especially around the greens, where his precision with the pitching clubs combined with a few providential bounces to save a total of six shots, just enough for a one-stroke victory over Jack Nicklaus.

Yet it was not Nicklaus but Tony Jacklin who suffered most acutely

from Trevino's strokes of magic. For two days Jacklin played head-to-head with the Merry Mex, matching him birdie for birdie and waiting to take the upper hand. On the seventy-first hole it seemed his time had come.

The par-five seventeenth was bad news for Trevino, even before he struck his first shot. With his ball on the tee and his mind set on "go," Lee was jolted when a cameraman crossed in front of the teeing area. It completely unsettled him, and he complained loudly to officials before getting back to business. In truth he never calmed down completely, for he pulled his tee shot into the depths of a fairway bunker.

Jacklin seized the opportunity and delivered a long, hard drive, thirty yards past Trevino's and dead in the center of the fairway.

Still muttering to himself about the photographer, Trevino wedged weakly from the bunker, advancing the ball a few yards down the fairway, but still not up to Jacklin's drive. He then pulled his three-wood shot into a hill of heavy rough, fifty feet short and left of the green. Jacklin hit a similar shot, but got it past Trevino's and onto level land.

As Trevino stepped to his wedge shot, it seemed that the anger had mellowed into melancholy. He played quickly and perhaps carelessly, catching the ball thin and sending it through the green several feet up a grassy bank. Now he had taken four strokes, and each of them had pulled him farther from the trophy. Jacklin, lying two, surely would gain one shot, possibly two and, in all likelihood, given Trevino's state of mind, three.

Trevino stared blankly back at the tee as Jacklin settled on his ball. "I was so hot about that photographer, I couldn't think of anything else, except

that I had lost the championship," Trevino recalls.

Jacklin's pitch was rather weak and left him perhaps twenty feet away from a birdie. Still, he was well inside Trevino, who faced a ticklish downhill chip. Normally Lee would have stalked the shot carefully, but, still visibly discouraged, he simply stepped up and gave the ball a listless nudge. But a listless nudge was apparently what the ball needed. It flopped onto the edge of the green, trickled forward and dropped smack into the center of the cup for a par five.

For a moment Jacklin sat stunned on the bank of the green, the roar of the gallery echoing in his ears. Then he walked to his ball.

"I'll hole this one and still go to eighteen one up," he told himself. But he was too aggressive and perhaps too shaken. The putt went nearly three feet past the cup.

"I wasn't really worried about the one coming back," he said, "but I got quick on the putt through lack of concentration—though really the circumstances had more to do with it than anything else—and I missed it. By tenfold that was the worst shock I've ever had on a golf course."

Incredibly, Trevino had *gained* a stroke. With his back to the ropes he had delivered the knock-out blow. Momentum and confidence restored, he birdied the final hole as the decimated Jacklin bogeyed to finish third behind Nicklaus. Years later Jacklin remarked, "Nothing really good ever happened to me after Muirfield."

Charge Your Chips

Trevino's victory at Muirfield makes two very important points about the game of golf. First, you should never give up, no matter how bleak the situation. And, secondly, the difference between first place and second is a confident short game.

Golf instruction has traditionally emphasized the importance of "getting up and down," of "converting three shots into two."

But why be so conservative? Remember, most chip shots are no more difficult than long putts, and many are easier. Most golfers try to sink all their putts, so why not also try to sink your chip shots? At least you should "think sink" as you plan and address these shots. Gary Player takes that attitude on his sand shots, and he is one of the finest bunker players the game has ever seen.

If you charge your chips, the worst thing you'll do is hit a few of them past the hole, but at the same time you'll leave fewer short of the hole. That alone is a good thing, because the more chips that reach the hole, the greater the chances of some going in. So forget about "up and down" and concentrate on "in." Just adopting the "think sink" philosophy will help you increase your quota of hole-outs.

Of course, even the most positive attitude will be of little help if you don't have the proper mechanics. So here is a review of the basics of an aggressive chipping technique.

The first rule is to get the ball rolling smoothly on the green as soon as possible. A rolling chip is much easier to gauge and predict than a lofted shot, so your object is to fly the ball just over the fringe and then let it roll most of its way to the hole.

The second rule is to know your irons. If you use the same chipping stroke on your four-iron and sand-wedge, the ball will react differently. With the four-iron it will shoot off quickly and roll a long way. With the wedge it will have a lot more loft, a lot less pace and will roll less than half the distance of the four-iron chip. So the four-iron is best when you have relatively little fringe to clear but you need lots of roll, and the sand-wedge is called for when you have several feet of fringe to clear but must stop the ball relatively quickly. Of course, each of the clubs between the four-iron and sand-wedge reacts a little differently, so practice with all your irons around the green and learn how each club makes the ball react. Once you know that, chipping becomes simply a matter of matching the club to the situation.

Now, let's say you're three feet from the green, you have twenty-five feet to the hole and you've decided the seven-iron is your club. Your next task is to visualize the ideal shot. Decide where you want the ball to land and how you want it to roll to the pin—and be *specific*. How many bounces will it take? What sort of break will it have? Be particularly careful in judging the last few feet of roll, because at that point the ball will be moving very slowly and will be more susceptible to the pitch and grain and speed of the green. When your inspection is concluded you should be able to visualize the ideal shot from the moment the ball leaves the club through touchdown on the green and its roll along the putting surface to its final plop into the hole. You *must* have this vision before you go any farther or you'll have little hope of sinking the chip.

As to chipping technique, shorten your grip at least two or three inches, because the closer your hands are to the ball, the more touch and control you'll have (as fine a short game player as Hubert Green grips down right to the metal). Take an open stance, with your left foot three or four inches removed from the target line and your hips and shoulders also aligned well to the left. Your stance should be narrow —so narrow that your heels are no more than four or five inches apart. Position the ball off your left heel so that your right toe is pointing directly at it. Your posture should have two checkpoints: You should stand straight enough so that your arms are fully extended but bend over enough so that your nose is directly above the ball. About seventy percent of your weight should be on your left side.

If you set up in this position, your hands will be three or four inches ahead of the clubface. During the stroke this leading position of the hands should be maintained. The best chipping stroke is one in which the arms and hands do most of the work, with the wrists cocking only slightly and reflexively.

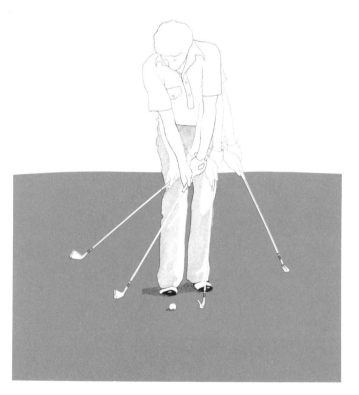

The stance is narrow and open, and the stroke is made with the arms and hands.

The backswing is similar to the takeaway for a full shot—just a slow, low motion about two feet back from the ball. At the end of the backswing you may allow your wrists to cock slightly, but not much. The club should not rise more than a foot or so off the ground. In the forwardswing, keep the hands leading the clubface as you come through the ball. By minimizing wrist action and "holding the angle," you'll maintain the same "radius" you set at address, and virtually eliminate fat and topped shots. The ball will take off low, crisply and on line.

Assuming that you do hit your chip shots crisply and on line, there is plenty of reason to leave the flag in the hole. Some golfers are fond of saying "the flag never knocks a ball in," but it sure has converted some overly strong chips to winners. Look at it this way: On a long putt, you can't really be aggressive because you aren't allowed to keep the pin in. On the chip you *can* have this added advantage, so why not take it? It can be a welcome backstop. The only time to take the pin out is when it leans toward you and obviously blocks the ball from going into the hole.

The final tip is to take a few practice swings before each chip shot. Every chip is unique and demands proper feel and confidence, so prepare yourself for a firm and positive stroke by getting that feel. As you take your practice strokes, continue to visualize the ideal chip rolling dead into the cup. Then, just address the ball and let it happen, as Lee Trevino did.

IF YOU DARE: SPIN YOUR CHIPS

Once you have perfected the standard chipping method, you can learn to make the ball "dance" a bit—hit high shots that stop, low shots that stop, high that run, low that run. Such variety helps you adjust to any greenside situation. Your ball position dictates trajectory; move the ball up in your stance and you'll get a higher shot, move it back for a lower shot. By rotating your hands counterclockwise a quarter-turn as you grip the club, you'll create a weak "slicer's grip." This, combined with a slightly open clubface at address and an outward takeaway, will produce a shot with backspin and slicespin, a shot that will fly a bit higher and stop more quickly than a normal chip. Taking a "hook grip"—with the hands rotated a quarter-turn clockwise—and making a slightly inside takeaway with a bit of wrist action, will produce an extremely low, fast-running shot.

Here's a quick-reference guide that shows you how to use the ball position and hook-slice techniques to play all sort of chip shots:

Shot Needed	Ball Position	Grip and Swing	Clubface and Club
Very high with stop	forward	slice	open; wedge
High with stop	forward	normal	square; wedge
Low with run	back	normal	square; five-iron
Very low with run	back	hook	square; five-iron
High with run	forward	hook	square; nine-iron
Low with stop	well back	slice	square; seven-iron

BEN HOGAN
at the U.S. Open

The cut shot

With singleminded dedication, Ben Hogan made himself the best striker of a golf ball the world has ever seen. And he did so twice.

During the 1930's the young Texan struggled against his own uniquely mechanical style—a strong grip, a long, wide, flat backswing and a powerful lash through impact with the arms and hands. That volatile sequence of movements, when not executed in complete harmony, produced Hogan's ballistic nemesis—the uncontrolled hook.

But he made it work, through practice—more practice than most humans could endure. Ten-hour sessions were not uncommon. And he hit not hundreds but tens of thousands of balls, until his hands bled, or until the shots were launching, flying and landing the way he wanted.

It was nearly a decade before Hogan took his first professional title, the 1940 North-South Open at Pinehurst. But things came together quickly after that. In 1940 he won five times and was the tour's leading money winner, taking the Vardon Trophy as well. In 1941 he again won five times, again led the money list and again won the Vardon Trophy. And in 1942 it was the same, except that he won not five events but six.

After three years in the Army Air Corps, Hogan returned quickly to form. From 1946 to 1948 he won thirty-three events. It was during this post-war era that Hogan also began to correct his fatal swing flaw. With the practice tee as his laboratory, he tested and retested every flick, hitch and sway until he arrived at the perfect formula—a shortened thumb position, an opened stance and a pronated arm swing that gave him a fade. And truly this was not just *any* fade, but the most controlled and dependable fade the game had ever seen. He had lost a bit of distance, to be sure, but had more than compensated for it with uncommon accuracy.

In 1948 Hogan raised his powers to their ultimate height, winning eleven tournaments including the U.S. Open and the PGA. A year later it seemed his career was over, when, returning from a tournament to his home in Ft. Worth, his car collided with a bus.

They said he would never play again, but they didn't know Hogan. A few months later he forced his battered body back to the practice range, and a few months after that he entered—and won—the 1950 U.S. Open at Merion.

In one year, he worked as hard on his swing as he had in the two previous decades. The rebuilt motion was a softer, less crashing style, yet it retained the essential Hogan rhythm, the rigid grace that one writer likened to a "machine stamping out bottle caps."

In the years that followed Hogan won sixteen more events, including three more U.S. Opens, two Masters and a British Open—all the while battling a balky putter.

The fact was that no one could put the ball into the fairway more surely or consistently than Hogan. And once on the short grass he rarely failed to find the green. To this day, weekend golfers boast when they make a "Hogan four": center of the fairway, center of the green, down in two.

Added to this accuracy was Hogan's conservative manner and cold concentration on the course. "Golf is twenty percent technique and eighty percent management," he once said, and he managed himself carefully. He was rarely seen to play a daring or desperate shot. That was fine for the other champions—the Hagens, the Sneads, the rest of the crowd. But not for the Hawk. He didn't have to go after birdies—they came to him.

However, there was at least one occasion late in his career when Hogan decided to break his own battle plan—

at Cherry Hills in 1960. It was Ben's last real opportunity to win a record fifth U.S. Open, and as the fourth round drew to a close he seemed on the verge of doing it. With two holes to go he was tied with the only other man capable of winning the championship, Arnold Palmer. In those days the Open concluded with thirty-six holes on Saturday, and Hogan played flawlessly all day, hitting each of the first thirty-four greens in regulation. But now he needed a birdie, and this par five was where he would have to make it.

Hogan lined out a perfect drive and an equally perfect second shot to position himself sixty yards short of the pin. But it was a treacherous sixty yards. The seventeenth green at Cherry Hills is an island, encircled by a small, menacing creek. On that final day the flag was cut not fifteen feet from the edge of the water.

Hogan's options were to pitch safely past the pin, risking a long roll on the fast green, or to try to loft the ball to the edge of the green so that it would settle tight to the hole. The latter, of course, meant flirting with the water.

He knew from the beginning that a "good" shot would not be good enough. Palmer, a hole back and playing his usual aggressive game, could be expected to gun for a birdie. Hogan would have to do the same.

A soft breeze was blowing into his face as his wedge clipped the ball neatly into the air. At first the little shot looked perfect, and the crowd began to roar in anticipation. But their cheers suddenly turned to gasps, and then to an eerie hush, as the ball landed a foot short of the green and bounded backward into the moat.

Five minutes later Hogan waded in the water, his right trouser leg rolled to the knee. He was able to blast the ball onto the green, but left himself thirty feet past the hole. From there he two-putted. The bogey six sent him to the final hole trailing Palmer by a shot.

That was the end. Apparently unsettled by his disaster, Hogan pulled his tee shot into the lake at eighteen and finished in a tie for ninth place, four strokes behind Palmer.

The Cut Shot

The cut is the height of shotmaking finesse. As such, it is not easy to play perfectly, as Hogan's story proves. Miss it even slightly and you can pay heavily. However, with practice you can learn to hit this shot consistently, and, when you do, you'll see just how useful it is. First, it can help you flick the ball over a bunker or make it sit softly on a hard green. And when you drop the ball close to the hole from a difficult lie, you will get a psychological boost (or deliver an unexpected blow to your opponent). So the cut shot is well worth learning.

The principle involved in hitting the cut shot is the same as for the intentional slice. Basically, you cut across the ball from outside-to-in to put left-to-right spin on the ball. When you do that with a straight-faced club the ball makes a big bend to the right, but when you do it with a wedge you simply increase the backspin on the ball so that it rises quickly and sits soon after it hits the green.

Take your wedge and address the ball with a wide-open stance—knees, hips and shoulders all facing at least thirty degrees left of your target. Your left foot should be flared so that your toe is pointing just right of where you want to land the ball. On a flat green the left-to-right spin on the ball will cause it to bounce to the right, so compensate by aiming a few feet left of your target.

The clubface should be laid flat back and open, aimed fifteen to twenty degrees to the right of your target. Play the ball off your left toe so that your hands are just in back of the ball. This will increase the effective loft on the club.

The swing is an exaggerated form of the slice swing. Use an outside takeaway—swing your arms along the line on which you've aligned your body,

Body alignment is wide open, with everything pointing at least 30 degrees left of target.

or even outside that line a bit if possible. Also, take the club up quickly with an early cocking of the wrists. Since it's important to make very accurate contact on this shot, keep the swing "quiet," with a minimum of weight shift and a short, controlled backswing. On the downswing, just concentrate on slipping the club under the ball. Don't try to scoop it up. Let the clubhead do all the lifting work.

When the lie is lush, your sand-wedge is the best club to use because its loft will give you maximum height and the softest possible landing. However, the sand-wedge can be dangerous from tight lies, where the ball sits low to the ground. You may not be able to slip its broad flange under the ball. In such cases, it's best to use a pitching-wedge.

Use a wristy backswing, but keep the swing controlled and evenly paced.

The shot will kick to the right after it lands, so compensate by aiming a bit left of the target.

IF YOU DARE: LOB IT

Picture two-time Open winner Julius Boros playing a short pitch shot, and you'll have a good idea of how to play the lob. The lob in golf is similar to the overspin lob in tennis—a long, lazy, arching shot that flies high and then bounces forward quickly. It is best used when you have to hit a high shot to the pin over an obstacle, and it's also useful from the rough as an effective alternative to the cut shot. The shot is played almost exclusively with the sand-wedge.

Take an open stance, square the club to your target and play the ball off your left instep. Then take the laziest swing you can. Bobby Jones once said that "nobody ever swung a golf club too easily." On the lob shot, you must try to make Jones a liar. Just take the club back as deliberately as you can while maintaining feel and control. Then drop it down and through the ball.

"Dead-hand" the shot, keeping your wrists stiff throughout the swing, thus insuring that the clubface is fully lofted as it passes through impact. The result on a shot of, say, fifty feet should be a high, soft floater that lands about two-thirds of the way to the pin, bounces softly and rolls forward the rest of the way. Like the cut, the lob is a shot that requires feel and finesse, two things which come only after lots of practice.

BILLY CASPER
at the U.S. Open

The punch shot

Back in 1957, Ben Hogan is reputed to have looked Billy Casper in the eye and, with characteristic bluntness, told him, "If you couldn't putt you'd be selling hot dogs on the tenth tee."

In his prime, Billy Casper could indeed putt. It is possible he was the best the game has ever seen. And his ability was never more evident than in the 1959 U.S. Open at Winged Foot, where he staged the most sensational display of putting in the history of that championship, using only 114 strokes in 72 holes over 18 of the world's most difficult greens.

When a golfer's putting is "on," as Casper's was that week, it takes a lot of pressure off the tee-to-green game. Yet, ironically, when a string of one-putt greens begins to grow, one starts to wonder just how long the magic will last, and the pressure starts to fold back on itself. That is what happened to Casper in the final round at Winged Foot.

In those days the Open concluded with thirty-six holes on Saturday, but at Winged Foot heavy rains forced postponement of the final eighteen for twenty-four hours. When play started on Sunday the weather still had not cleared. The sky was as gray as the old stone clubhouse, the temperature was in the low 50's, and a strong blustery wind blew across the fairways, wreaking havoc with everyone's scores.

Casper had finished his Saturday round by one-putting the last three holes for a 69 and a 54-hole total of 208. Three strokes behind him was Hogan, and one farther back were Arnold Palmer, Sam Snead and Bob Rosburg.

Billy began the day by missing the green at the first hole, wedging up to about four feet and sinking the putt. That set the pattern for the early part of his round. On the second he drove into a fairway bunker, again missed the green with his approach, but again pitched to within ten feet and sank the putt for a par. On the short third the wind pushed his teeshot several yards to the right of the green, but again he flipped a wedge over a bunker and sank a curling nine-footer for par. His approach to the fourth hole plugged into the face of a bunker, but he blasted to seven feet and again in went the putt. On the par-five fifth he reached the green in three and then canned a twenty-footer for a birdie. He was then one under for five holes, and yet had hit only one green in regulation. Counting Saturday's finish, he had one-putted eight straight holes. How much longer could he survive on this brand of scrambling golf?

The answer came on the next hole, a short but deceptively difficult par four that was playing into the face of a forty-mile-per-hour wind. Under normal conditions number six was a drive and a flip wedge, even from the championship tees, but on that Sunday in June the second shot had become suddenly awesome. The green was the shallowest target on the course, and the USGA demons had placed the flagstick in the shallowest part of it, directly in back of a smiling guardian bunker.

Despite the wind, Casper nailed his drive into the heart of the fairway, leaving just over a hundred yards to the pin. On the three previous days he had lofted a wedge tight to the hole, posting two birdies and a par, but now the wedge was not enough. Instead, he chose a nine-iron, opting to punch the ball at the pin.

It was an easy shot to miss. Too little power, and the wind would bat the ball down into the bunker. Too much power, and he could bound off the back of the green and into heavy rough—U.S. Open rough. Either way, it would be a near-certain bogey, and would continue to pressure his short

game. Still, he knew that a well-played punch shot would stand up to the wind, land softly and hold the green—something he had been trying to do all day without success.

With customary dispatch, Casper set his feet and rocked into a low, handsy backswing, then pulled briskly down and through. The ball darted off low and straight, then climbed upward into the face of the wind. It cleared the bunker and fell almost straight down onto the green, twelve feet from the hole.

Finally, a solid approach shot, a shot that did what he wanted it to do. The skid had ended. But so, ironically, had the hot putting. Casper missed the birdie, settling for a regulation two-putt par. Under the circumstances, however, that was the finest kind of par a man could make.

"That little punch was the best shot I hit all day," Casper recalls, "It restored my confidence in my ability to handle the course, not just the greens, and it set the tone for the rest of the round." Steady golf from that point on gave him a one-stroke edge over Bob Rosburg for the biggest victory of his career.

The Punch Shot

The punch can save you strokes even if you never find yourself playing into a forty-mile-per-hour wind to a shallow green in the U.S. Open.

The shot can be played with any club from the seven-iron to the pitching-wedge, but the nine-iron is generally the best choice, giving the most control yet not too much loft.

Play the ball about midway between your feet from a square or slightly open stance. Your hands should be ahead of the ball and seventy percent of your weight should be on your left side. Also, be sure to grip

The ball is well back in the stance, and roughly 70 percent of your weight is left.

Lead through impact with the left hand, and keep your finish very low.

down on the shaft of the club at least two inches.

The shot is aptly named a "punch" because it is played almost entirely with the arms. There is relatively little lower body movement, and wrist action is also kept to a minimum. Take the club back with your arms, allowing a natural response from your wrists and legs, to a point where your hands are just short of shoulder-height. From that point, swing down and through briskly with the arms, being sure that the right hand does not roll over the

left as you come into impact. Do not make any lateral moves with the lower body and do not flick with the wrists.

The finish to this shot is important. Keep the club low and point it toward the target. You shouldn't allow your hands to rise any higher than your belt.

The ball will bore on a low trajectory. Into heavy wind it will rise slightly, then plummet straight down. By the time it reaches the green there is almost no backspin on the shot, and so it sits wherever it hits.

IF YOU DARE: PUNCHES THAT BEND

Once you develop some confidence with the punch shot, it's relatively easy to make the ball draw and fade on a low trajectory. For cut and draw punches, it's best to use a choked down seven-iron because this club has less loft than a nine-iron and you can more readily apply the sidespin that makes the ball turn right or left. To hit a punch fade, simply open your stance wide, then use the same swing used for the punch, but try to feel as if you are cutting the ball at impact, swinging across from outside to inside. If that doesn't work, add another adjustment: weaken your grip at address by rolling both hands counterclockwise a quarter turn so that the "V's" formed by your thumbs and forefingers point at your chin. Then use the swing just described. To hit a punch draw, close the stance slightly so that your toe line, knees, hips and shoulders are aligned a few yards right of your target. Take the club back inside, and as you come through the ball let the wrists roll. Sam Snead describes the proper feel in the wrists as "oily" as they flip through impact, closing the clubface and imparting the counterclockwise spin that makes the ball draw. Remember on both shots to keep your finish low, with the clubhead pointing straight out toward the flag.

SEVE BALLESTEROS

at the British Open

The pitch and run

In the 120-year history of the British Open, only two "kids" have challenged for the title. The first was Tom Morris, Jr., who won the first of four consecutive Open championships in 1868, at age seventeen. The second youth did not appear until more than a century later, when in 1976 at Royal Birkdale a handsome nineteen-year-old Spaniard led the field for the first three rounds. He didn't win the title that year, but through his spectacular play he served notice that he would soon return for the trophy. His name was Severiano Ballesteros.

Few had heard of him prior to that Wednesday in July when he fired a course record 69 to share the first-round lead. "He's the nephew of Ramon Sota, the old Spanish pro," said someone in the gallery. "I hear he has three brothers already in the game," said someone else. And by nightfall the talk was that Ballesteros had come from a poor family, grown up in a farmhouse on the northern Spanish coast and had learned the game as

a caddie. It was all true, and by week's end the Ballesteros story was Topic A among golfers throughout the world.

In the second round the youngster seemed to falter early, but then blistered the back side in 31, birdieing seventeen and eighteen for his second straight 69. His 138 total gave him a share of the lead with Johnny Miller.

Early in the third day it looked as if Ballesteros would crack. His drives, which had not been models of accuracy all week, really began to sail, often so far afield that he needed several spectators to help in the search. But he was always long—longer than anyone else—and somehow he was always able both to find the ball and to recover miraculously from the heather and gorse. On several occasions he converted certain bogeys into stupefying birdies.

Ballesteros was giving the British fans the first taste of a swashbuckling style of play that has now become familiar the world over. Hit it hard, find it and hit it hard again. Then knock it down the throat of the cup. To hell

127

with percentage golf—let others steer the ball nervously over the short grass. Seve gambled first and worried later. Not since Arnold Palmer had the game seen skill, luck and panache blended so favorably in a young player.

In the third round Ballesteros hit only four fairways, yet he scrambled, blasted, chipped and putted his way to a 73, two better than his playing partner, Miller, who posted an inglorious 75.

On the day of reckoning Ballesteros quickly increased his lead to three when, on the first hole, he made another fairwayless, greenless par to Miller's bogey.

But that was the end. In the next eight holes Ballesteros' errant play caught up with him as he returned five pars, two bogeys and a double bogey. Miller, regaining briefly the brilliance of Oakmont, played the same stretch in two under par, thereby converting a three-stroke deficit to a three-stroke lead.

On the back nine Seve continued to stumble as Miller birdied twelve and eagled thirteen. With five holes left the lead was an insurmountable eight shots.

Although the title was now out of reach, Seve wanted to finish well. Jack Nicklaus had posted a 275, and with a few more birdies the young Spaniard could equal that score. He gathered himself, and from fourteen in played strong golf. A birdie on fourteen, pars on fifteen and sixteen, and then a welcome eagle on seventeen. Now just one more birdie on the final par five would tie him with Nicklaus.

With thousands in the grandstands cheering him on, Seve hit a long but leaky teeshot that drifted into light rough. On his second shot he swung too hard and pulled the ball left, pin high but fenced from the green by

two menacing pot bunkers. Miller, enjoying the certainty of a six-shot victory, strode triumphantly through the throng, his putter held high in the air, while off to the side of the green Ballesteros studied one of the most perplexing situations he had ever faced.

The pin was cut extremely close to the near edge of the green, and the greens had been lightning-fast and unpredictable all week. If he chose to hit a high, soft shot, he could not keep the ball within ten feet of the hole, no matter how delicately he lobbed it. The other alternative was a frightening one —he could try to skittle the ball *between* the bunkers. There was an alley perhaps three feet wide, and at the end of it was the flagstick. But the terrain was rough and broken from four days of steady trampling—even a well-played shot could easily hit an uneven spot and kick right or left into jail. From there a birdie would be impossible, and even a par doubtful.

Ballesteros did not dwell on the negatives. As Miller chipped up and holed the winning putt, Seve drew his nine-iron and began plotting his gamble. The crowd quieted for this, the final episode of the championship and the most important shot in the Spaniard's young career.

With the touch of a safecracker he sent the ball bravely out across the uneven turf. It bounced once, twice, three times, but held its line, passing safely between the bunkers. Just at the fringe it lost some of its pace, and drifted slowly across the green, stopping four feet from the hole.

Roughly three minutes later Ballesteros sank the putt for the birdie he needed to finish tied for second. Three years later he brought his flamboyant game back to England, this time to Royal Lytham and St. Annes, where he won the British Open. At twenty-two he was the youngest champion since Young Tom Morris.

The Bump-and-Run

Although the heavily-watered courses of America rarely force golfers to play running shots to the pin, the bump-and-run is still a useful shot to have in your repertoire, particularly if you play in the windy South or Southwest, and, naturally, for those vacation trips to the British Isles.

Don't try the pitch and run unless the terrain is relatively flat and unmarked.

The shot is played in much the same way as the basic chip described in chapter 18, the major difference being in reading and dealing with the terrain. On a normal chip you simply land the ball on the green and let it roll to the hole, but when you play a bump-and-run you must land the ball short of the green and let it bounce on. Thus the first step is to inspect the ground between yourself and the hole.

Is the terrain particularly bumpy? Are there lots of roots, stones and un-even areas? Is the grass longer than fairway grass? If so, you should think twice about playing a bump-and-run. In any case, your objective should be to land the ball on a relatively flat, unmarked area of turf, so that it bounces forward with the desired direction and pace.

Read the break as you would on a putt, and take into account any sideward kick the ball will get on its first or second bounce. Consider also the "speed" of the fringe and prefringe areas. The fringe particularly can take spin off a shot and leave it well short of the hole.

Finally, select the club that will loft the ball to the best possible landing area while also enabling you to reach the green. Generally, you will not use either of the wedges for pitch-and-run shots because they don't give you enough roll, but most of the other irons can be used, and certainly the four through nine.

More often than not, the bump-and-run must be played from a hilly lie. If you should have to play the ball from an uphill lie, be aware that you will tend to leave it short, and guard against that by taking one club more than you think you should—an eight-iron, for example, rather than a nine. Take the club back down the slope and hit briskly through the ball.

On downhill shots, take one club less, unless you want a lot of run, because downhill lies encourage a low, rolling shot. Stay down on the ball during the swing, and concentrate on contacting the ball before the club catches the slope. You can help yourself in that regard by placing ninety percent of your weight on your left side at address.

When you have a sidehill lie with the ball above your feet, shorten your grip even more than normal for a chip

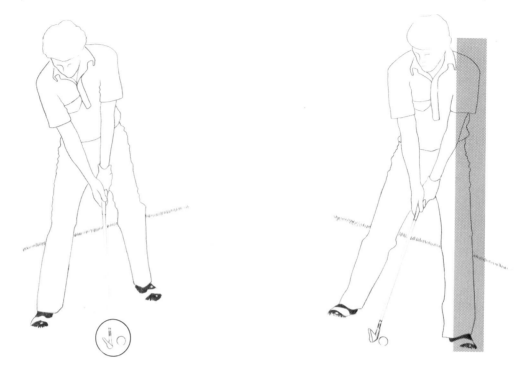

On an uphill lie, guard against leaving the ball short—take a less lofted club than usual. Playing downhill, use a more lofted club and shade 90 percent of your weight left.

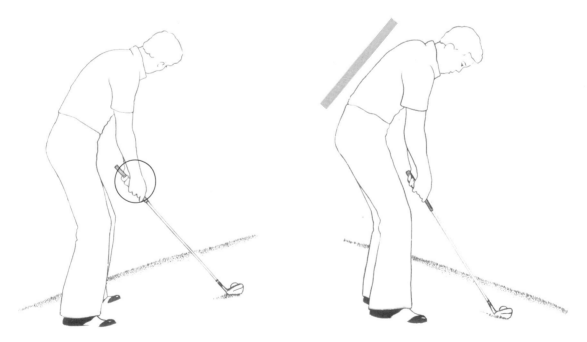

On a sidehill lie with the ball above your feet, grip down on the club. When the ball is below your feet, guard against a shank by standing slightly more erect than usual.

shot so that you avoid any tendency to stub the club. Also, aim to the right just a hair, because from this stance you will tend to pull the ball left. When the ball is below your feet you should guard against a shank; concentrate on keeping your weight back on your heels to avoid falling forward and thereby moving the club out toward the ball for a hoseled impact. A slightly more upright stance will also aid the cause. And, since you will have a tendency to push this shot to the right, close the blade a bit, and aim just a hair to the left of your intended target.

IF YOU DARE: "DEAD-HAND" IT

Occasionally around the green you'll get a lie that is so good it's bad. The ball sits up high on a tuft of grass, almost perched in air. Such lies make it very difficult to apply a crisp downward stroke to the ball as you normally would on a chip, and when you do make such an impact the ball tends to shoot out quickly as it does on a fairway shot hit from a grassy lie. A better solution is to "pop" the ball out with a dead-handed chip. To hit this pop chip, grip down on the club more than usual (remember that, since the ball is perched, it's closer to your hands than normal, and adjust accordingly). Address the ball carefully, holding the clubhead in the air behind the ball so as not to dislodge it and cause yourself a two-stroke penalty. Then simply hit a dead-handed chip, with the hands, wrists and arms all swinging together as if in a solid block. Take the club straight back from the ball and swing it straight through in a pendulum motion, slightly more slowly than you normally would though still with acceleration. This technique will "pop" the ball out of its perch, with a slightly higher trajectory than a chip. The ball will land quietly and will not scoot. For an even softer landing, play the shot with a slightly open clubface. You can vary the length of this shot simply by increasing the length and/or pace of your swing.

JOHNNY MILLER
at the World Open

The bank shot

When golf course architect Donald Ross designed his masterpiece, Pinehurst Number 2, he dotted the greenside areas with large grassy mounds. According to Ross, the mounds lent a flavor of the links courses of his native Scotland. But he had another reason as well.

"The mounding makes possible an infinite variety of nasty short shots that no other form of hazard can call for," he said. "Competitors whose second shots have wandered a bit will be disturbed by these innocent-appearing slopes and by the shots they will have to invent to recover."

In 1974, Johnny Miller learned the meaning of those words. At the absolute peak of his career, Miller came to Pinehurst for the $300,000 World Open, then the richest event in professional golf. At the time Miller was the tour's leading money winner with six victories and over $200,000 in prize money for the season. He had won the first three events of the year, then two more in the early spring. By mid-sea-

son he had begun to take long breaks from the tour, and there had been talk that perhaps he was no longer taking the game seriously. But then, two weeks before Pinehurst, Miller had put that kind of talk to rest with his sixth victory of the year in the Westchester Classic.

After three rounds at Pinehurst Miller shared the lead with Jack Nicklaus, his playing partner for the final day. Through the first few holes both men played steadily and they remained even. Then, on the difficult 438-yard fifth hole, Miller's approach flew over the back of the green and nestled among the mounds.

"I had a downhill lie on one mound and had to hit the shot over another mound to a fast, downhill-sloping green," says Miller. "Because the ball was lying badly and I had a tight pin position, a sand-wedge was out of the question; there was no way to stop the ball. Instead, I pulled out an eight-iron and decided to blast the ball right into the middle of the embankment."

It was a gamble, for if he was to hit the mound too low he would leave the ball in the heavy grass; and too high a shot would miss the mound altogether and run clear across the green. But, as he had all year, Miller played this delicate shot superbly. The ball pelted into the bank, hopped up, and slid down the green to within a foot of the hole. Miller made the putt for a par, went on to tie Nicklaus, Frank Beard and Bob Murphy in seventy-two holes, and then won the tournament, his seventh of the year, with a birdie on the second hole of the sudden-death playoff. Two weeks later he returned to his home in Napa, California, and won the Kaiser International with rounds of 69–69–67–66, capping one of the most successful seasons in modern golf history.

The Bank Shot

Good planning is the key to success on the bank shot. First, you must decide whether the shot is, indeed, the best choice. If the embankment is craggy, thickly grassed or wet, the bank shot is not a good idea, unless you have no other option. As with all pitch and chip shots, it's best to land the ball on firm, even ground. If the slope is extremely steep you will also have a tough time, because you'll have to hit the ball very hard in order to make the shot work, and when you start hitting a short shot very hard, you magnify the consequences of a mistake.

The bank shot poses a unique problem in that you must "land" the ball twice, once on the bank and once on the green or its fringe. Decide first where you want the ball to make its *second* bounce. Then, try to determine where you must hit the embankment in order to make the ball pop up and land on that second spot. Generally speaking, the higher you hit the ball on the bank, the harder you'll have to strike it, because you'll get less forward jump than if you strike near the bottom of the bank. A ball hit into the base of the bank may climb right up, but such a shot can be risky, and in most cases it's best to play for a firm hit into the center-to-top portion of the bank, which should produce a relatively "quiet" bounce. You can play the shot safely with any club from a five-iron to an eight-iron, and perhaps even a nine-iron or pitching-wedge, depending on your situation and style of play.

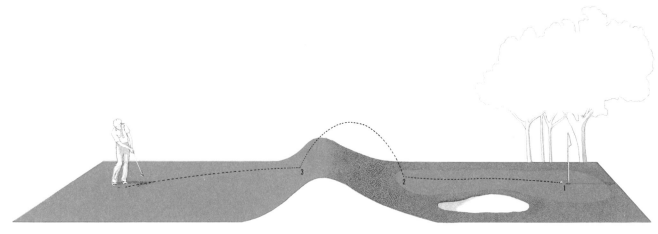

You will have two "landings," so gauge the shot carefully. Plan it "backward" from the hole, to the landing area on the green, to your target on the bank.

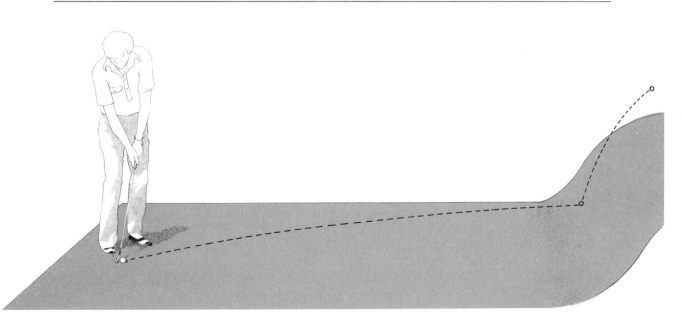

The shot is essentially a short, stiff-wristed punch, with any club from a five to eight iron. Try to land the ball into the center-to-top part of the bank, to get a "quiet" bounce.

Your choice should be determined by the height of your landing spot on the bank.

The shot you want is sort of a punched chip. Play the ball just back of center in a slightly open stance, and grip well down on the club, almost to the metal. Take a short, stiff-wristed backswing and sock the club sharply into the back of the ball.

IF YOU DARE: THE INTENTIONAL "FAT" SHOT

When you're faced with a bank shot or a tough cut shot over a bunker or other hazard, the intentional fat shot can often bail you out. The only requirement is that your ball be on relatively soft turf. The idea is to hit a bunker-type explosion shot, except that you use a pitching-wedge rather than a sand-wedge. By cutting into the ground behind the ball, you cushion your blow so that the ball rises softly upward and lands like the proverbial butterfly with sore feet. Play the ball about midway back in your wide-open stance. Close the face on the wedge slightly and then, using a short, wristy swing, bring the club down so that it digs into the ground two inches behind the ball. Most golfers have hit this shot unintentionally more times than they care to remember, but to play it on purpose takes some practice, so work on it before you test it in actual play.

TOM WATSON
at the Phoenix Open

The carom

As Tom Watson contemplated the chip shot that faced him, a shiver ran down his spine.

It was not a major championship, just the 1976 Phoenix Open. It was not the final round, only the third. And Watson was not leading the tournament—in fact, he was not even in contention. Nonetheless, this would be the most daring shot of his budding career —and for good reason. In one sense, his career was at stake.

Watson was on the fourteenth hole of the Phoenix Country Club. After a good drive, he had hit his second shot over the back of the green, down a small embankment, and within just a couple of feet of going out of bounds. In fact, what saved him was the brick wall which now prevented him from playing a normal third shot.

"My ball was too close to the wall for me to stand up to it and make a conventional swing," says Watson. "After trying to see if I could make a backswing, I considered taking an unplayable lie. But I was only ten yards or

so from the green and it seemed a shame to lose a shot so meekly. Then I thought of caroming the ball off the wall—actually hitting the ball at the wall, directly away from the green, and bouncing it back up the hill toward the hole.

"The more I looked at it, the better I liked the shot, and the riskier it seemed. First, this was not a standard brick wall. It was one of those decorative walls that have bricks missing every foot or so—and the holes left by the missing bricks were large enough for a golf ball to fly through. And, this brick wall was also uneven. There were jagged edges in the bricks, and if I were to hit one of them the ball might bounce anywhere.

"Then I started thinking about the places it might bounce into—such as me. If I were to hit myself, I'd be penalized two shots and if it then bounced off me and went back over the brick wall, it would be out of bounds. That would cost me another two strokes. But what *really* made me pause was the thought that, if the ball were to carom back into my hand or wrist, it could injure me seriously, maybe permanently.

"Still, I knew that if I hit the ball properly, and if the ball caromed properly, it would put me in far better position than I could ever hope to reach through a penalty drop or a bail-out shot of some kind. So I took out my nine-iron, calculated the angle I needed, tried to estimate the correct force, and gave it a rap."

It worked. The ball jolted cleanly off the wall, hit about halfway up the bank and climbed to the fringe of the green. From there Watson got down in two. He bogeyed the hole, but his gamble proved to be a good one.

Decide where you want the ball to finish, land and carom. Then ask yourself what club you will need to produce the shot you have visualized.

The Carom Shot

The ability to execute the carom derives not so much from physical touch as from mental alertness. First, you must have the imagination to "see" the shot. Too many golfers, when faced with a situation similar to the one Tom Watson encountered, fail to recognize the full range of possible shots. Many players simply yield to the rulebook, taking an unplayable lie and dropping (with one penalty shot) to a place from which they can swing freely. Others try to knock the ball out sideways, at a perpendicular angle to their target, usually gaining little and often putting themselves in a worse position than that from which they began.

So the first piece of instruction is to be imaginative, and keep your eyes and mind open to all the possibilities. The second tip is to know your rights. It could be that the object which impedes you is an immovable obstruction. If that's the case, you're entitled to relief, under Rule 31, 2c. A good golf club will list its immovable obstructions under "Local Rules," either on the scorecard or on a sign near the first tee.

In the event that you are not entitled to relief, take a good look at the obstruction before you decide to play the carom. Obviously, some materials make for better rebounds than others. Generally speaking, you shouldn't try to carom a ball off trees, wooden fences or wooden constructions of any kind, unless you have a very short distance to go. Even then, the tree carom is extremely risky because the rough bark surface can send the ball in any direction.

For the same reason stone walls or rough brick walls, such as the one Watson played off, are poor risks—especially if they have holes in them. The

ideal surface is smooth cement, with no angles, ridges or bumps.

Once you've decided to play the carom, play it carefully. Play the shot backward in your mind: Decide where you want the ball to stop, and then ask yourself where it must land in order to stop in that position. Finally, determine what sort of carom you must play in order to get the ball to that landing position. This will tell you the best club to use, how hard to swing and where to carom the ball on the object.

There are two things to keep in mind when actually playing this shot. First, be sure you align yourself in such a way that there is no chance the

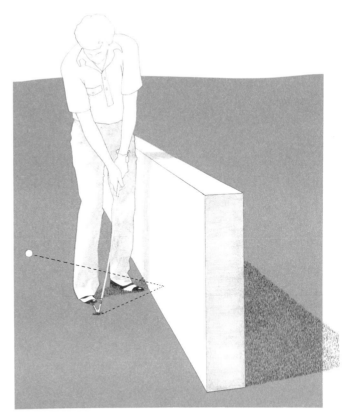

Try to eliminate your follow-through, to minimize the chance of the ball caroming into the club.

ball will hit you on the rebound. Second, try to hit the ball with more or less a descending blow, and, if possible, drive your iron down into the ground, with no follow-through. That will minimize the risk of the ball's hitting the clubface or shaft on the rebound.

Finally, don't expect perfection from this shot—remember, not even Watson got it onto the green. And don't get too anxious. Just give it a smooth stroke, containing your curiosity long enough that you stay down on the ball. Play this one well, and you'll have happy memories of it for a long time.

IF YOU DARE: THREE MORE OPTIONS

Occasionally you'll find yourself in a situation where your backswing is restricted, where you are not entitled to relief and where a carom shot is out of the question. For instance, your ball comes to rest near the base of a tree, and the tree is standing in the path of your backswing. You still have at least three options:

The One-handed Chop: Stand with your back to the target so that the ball is about five inches to the right of your right foot. Take a nine-iron or wedge, grip down to the metal, and square the clubface to the ball. Then chop down on it. For short shots, use a stiff-wristed pendulum swing; for longer shots, put some wrist into it.

The Left-handed Shot: There are two ways to hit this. The first is to take a two-iron and play the ball with the brand name side of the club. This is best for long or low shots. For shorter shots and those which must have loft, take a seven-iron, turn it upside down so that only the toe touches the ground and play the ball with the scored face. Regardless of which method you use, be sure to reverse hand positions, so that your left hand is below your right. Then just make a controlled swing, not too far back. You'll be surprised at the good results.

Between-the-Legs Shot: When a tree or other obstacle is in your swing path this is often the best ploy. Use a pitching-wedge and take a wide stance, about a foot-and-a-half from the ball, with your back toward the target and the ball dead-center between your legs. Square the club to your target line, then just lift it up and return it to the back of the ball with a deliberate downward chop. If played properly, it will take a couple of quick bounces and then speed along the ground like a rabbit.

TONY JACKLIN
at the U.S. Open

The pressure putt

Tony Jacklin was choking, and he knew it. As he started down the ninth fairway at Hazeltine Country Club, he could think only negative thoughts. The last two holes had been nightmares. Having dominated the 1970 U.S. Open for three-and-a-half rounds, he was suddenly in danger of losing everything—all because of two short putts.

"I was still leading, still a shot or two ahead of the pack, but I was beset with a thousand doubts. Two holes earlier, on number seven, I had hit a superb four-iron four feet from the hole. Then, incredibly, I missed the putt. It was bewildering. All week long I had putted so well, and then, on a putt that was a cinch, the ball slipped past the cup.

"It disoriented me, and I began to doubt myself. On the following hole, a par-three, I hit a two-iron to the back of the green, leaving a longish, downhill putt. My approach was weak and I faced another four-footer. This time I really worked carefully—and missed

again! Suddenly, the glue that had held me together had begun to rip me apart."

As Jacklin waited to hit his tee shot on number nine his mind raced back to Royal Lytham and St. Annes where, barely a year earlier, he had become the first Englishman in twenty years to win the British Open. Now he was on the verge of another historic achievement. If he could hold on for ninety minutes or so, he would be the first Briton since Tommy Armour to win the national championships of both Britain and the United States.

Of course, he had borne that special pressure from the beginning of the tournament, and all week long he had shown he deserved a place in the record books—until those two bedeviling putts.

The ninth at Hazeltine played 400 yards that day, with an extra narrow fairway and several bunkers guarding the green. Jacklin's desperate drive veered into long grass, from which he lashed almost vindictively with a four-iron. The ball cleared all the sand, but left him with a long putt straight up the face of the green.

Good players prefer such putts. When the stroke is smooth, an uphill putt lets the golfer control the ball and leaves comparatively little to chance, whereas a downhill putt is more subject to the pitch and speed of the green. But when one doubts one's stroke as Jacklin did at that moment, a straight uphill putt is the most terrifying assignment of all. Jacklin steeled himself with a threat: " 'It's now or never,' I told myself. 'Either you give this a good, solid, confident stroke, and start to get back on track, or you let yourself lose the Open, a victim of self-doubt.'

"The instant my putter touched the ball I said, 'My God, I've slammed it past the hole.' I can remember the crowd gasping at the force with which the ball shot up the slope. Surely it would sail six feet past, and I'd three-putt a third consecutive green. Then bingo—the ball hit the back of the hole, jumped three or four inches into the air and dropped right back into the cup for a birdie!

"No one can know the relief—and the renewed confidence—I felt when I saw that ball go in. It was precisely at that moment I knew the Open would be mine."

The key to a confident stroke is a confident read of the green. "See" the ideal putt.

The Pressure Putt

Putting has been called "the other game" within the game of golf because the skills it demands are so different from the requirements of the tee-to-green game. If it is, indeed, another game, then we may surely divide putting itself into two distinct varieties: normal putting and pressure putting.

Just as there are fine strikers of the ball who are terrible putters, there are fine putters who are hopelessly poor pressure putters. Traditionally,

when we think of pressure putting we imagine a "kneeknocker," a short putt that sends spasms through the hands and arms. But pressure putts can be of any length, as Tony Jacklin's story demonstrates. It all depends upon the situation in the match or tournament, and on the golfer. Each of us has a different pressure threshold, a point at which we feel the importance of the situation, and each of us reacts differently to that feeling. Some golfers feel it on the very first green, and then yip and choke all through the round. Others never feel it until the eighteenth, when they rise to the pressure and ram in the five-footer that wins the match.

Pressure putting requires both mental and physical discipline, and more of the former than the latter. As with normal putting, the physical technique is largely a matter of individual comfort. Comfort gives you confidence, and confidence is the only guaranteed weapon against pressure.

Yet, there are certain fundamentals which, if followed carefully, can help you to develop a pressure-resistant stroke. These fundamentals, combined with the proper attitude, will make you a good pressure putter.

The first fundamental is to keep your grip on the club relatively loose. When you make the mistake of tightening your grip, you also tighten the muscles in your hands and arms. That will inhibit your ability to take the club back smoothly and make an evenly ac-

celerating stroke. Instead, you'll jerk the putter back and then "yip" it through.

When the pressure is on the putt, take it off your grip. Hold it with just enough firmness to control it. You'll find that this not only gives you a smoother, more controlled stroke but also heightens your feel of the clubhead.

As to the stroke, there is good reason to believe that the most pressure-proof putting method is the stiff-wristed stroke. Many of the best putters in history—Bob Charles, Ben Crenshaw, George Archer, Dave Stockton—use an absolutely stiff-wristed, pendulum method, and most of the top pros, such as Jack Nicklaus and Tom Watson, use only minimal wrist movement.

There are good reasons for this. By keeping the hands and wrists relatively

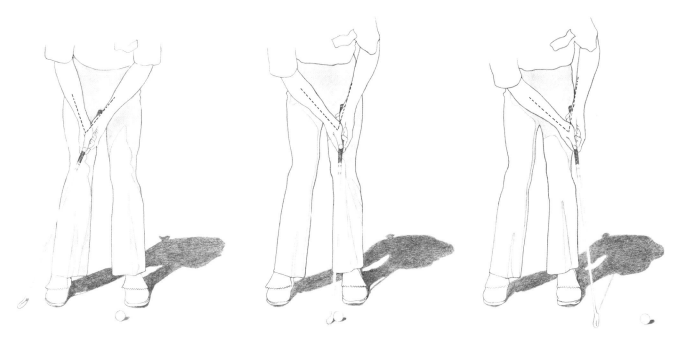

There are good reasons to adopt the stiff-wristed stroke used by most Tour pros. You minimize the moving parts and thereby insure a stroke that is less affected by nervous twitches.

motionless during the stroke you minimize the number of moving parts and thereby decrease the chance of throwing the putter off its proper swing path. In pressure putting, the wrists are the parts of the body most susceptible to nervous twitches and jerks, so by keeping them stiff you'll help stifle the yips.

Just pretend you are putting with your arms, wrists and hands in a double cast. When you address the ball, your arms will create a "Y" with the putter and your objective should be to maintain that "Y" throughout the stroke. The best way to do this is to control the swing entirely with your arms and shoulders. If you are not naturally a wrist putter, this shoulder swing will be difficult at first—you'll have a real temptation to flip at the ball. But with time you'll find that it produces a particularly smooth stroke.

Experiment with your ball position. Since this is a pendulum stroke, you'll have to be sure the putterhead contacts the ball at the exact bottom of its swing. So move the ball up and back in your stance until you find it is in the perfect spot.

Once you master the mechanics of this stroke, it becomes very easy to adjust the length of your putts simply by increasing and decreasing the length of your pendulum swing. The longer your swing, the farther the ball will roll.

IF YOU DARE: THINK "BEYOND"

The worst mistake you can make on a pressure putt is to leave it short. So when calculating the force with which to hit your putts, think "beyond." Try to strike the ball so that it has enough pace to roll one foot past the cup. This method will help you immediately by eliminating one way of missing the putt (leaving it short). Perhaps more important, an aggressive roll will restore your faith in yourself. Striking the ball firmly rather than "wishing" it to the hole will let you rely on your stroke and will help you to think of yourself as an overpowering putter by buoying your confidence. So, think one foot beyond, and, as you stroke the ball, visualize it not so much dropping but actually running into the hole the way a rabbit dives into its hutch.